NYRKR

Dot Shot it

Being born in New York is like hitting the lotto on your first try.

Here's why...

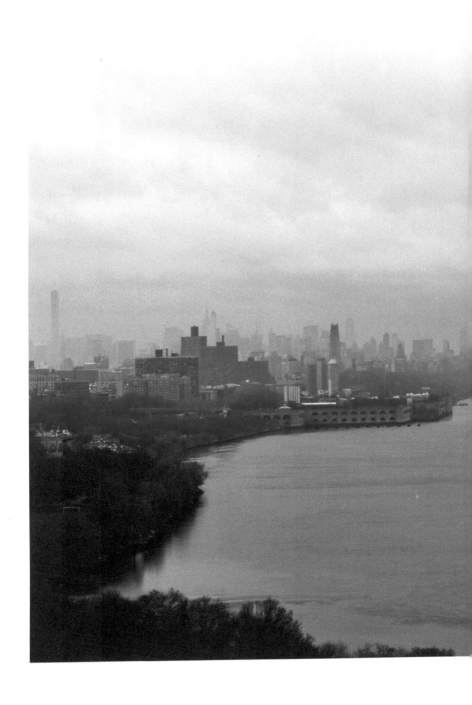

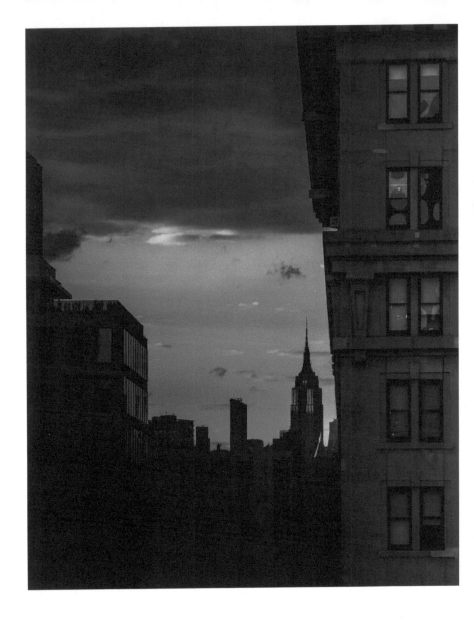

06·04·18 DUMBO

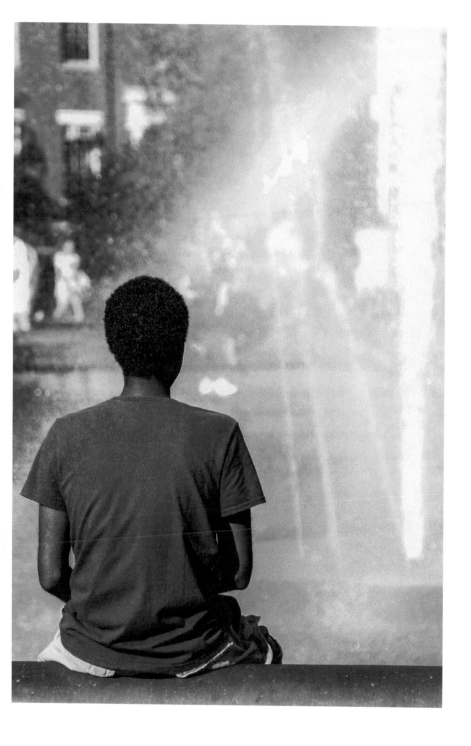

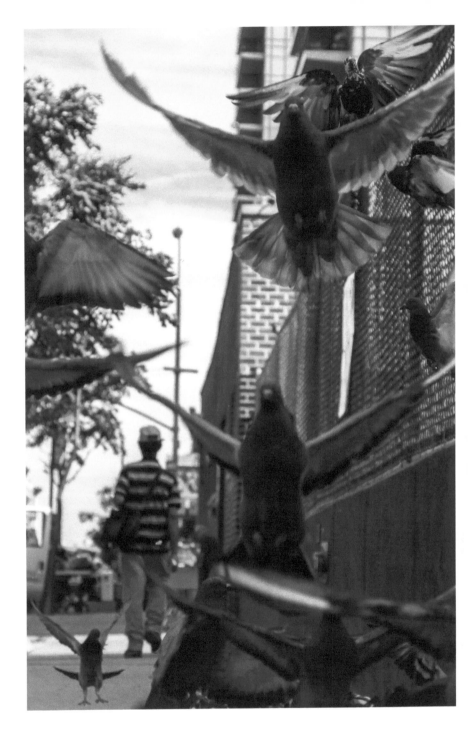

08-28-17 Washington Heights

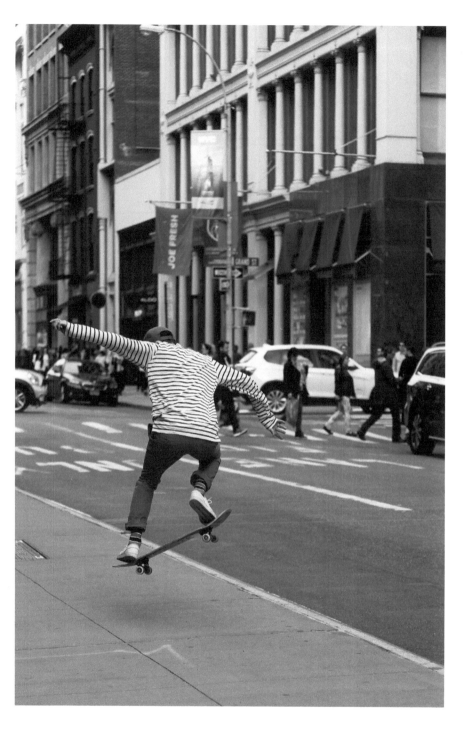

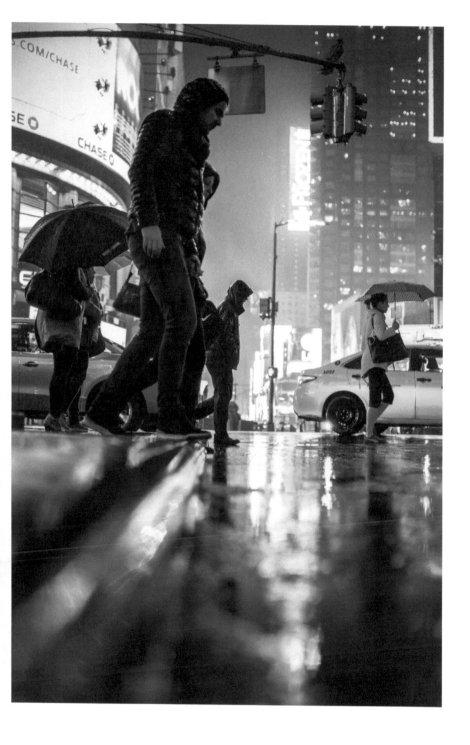

12-05-17 Times Square

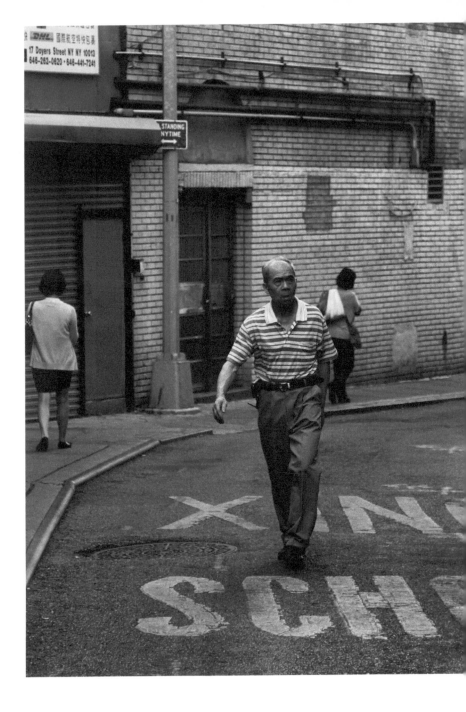

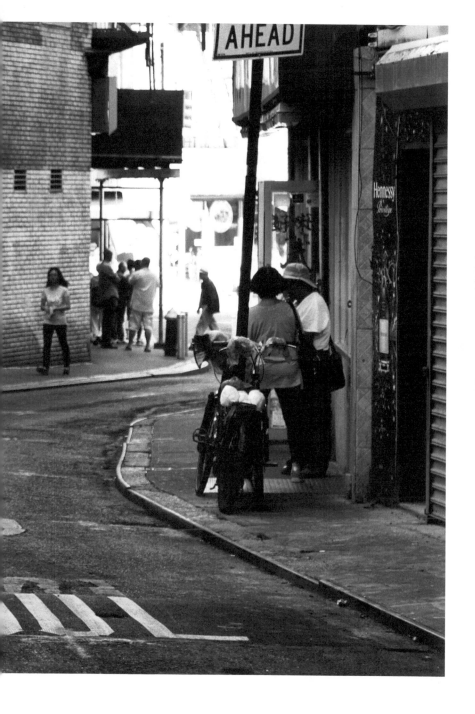

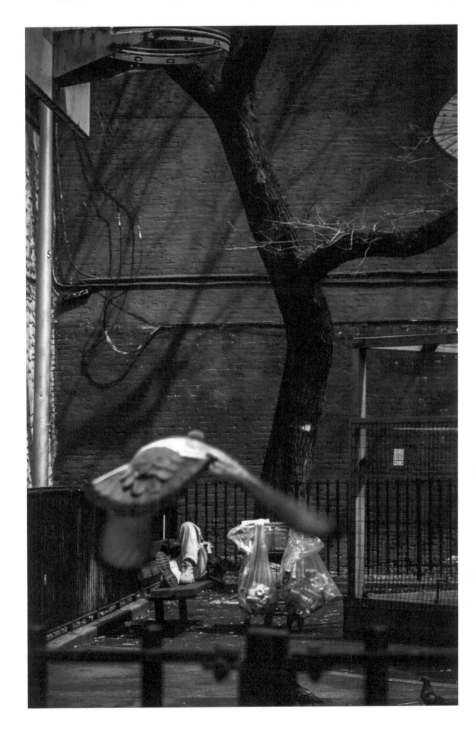

04-12-18 Chelsea

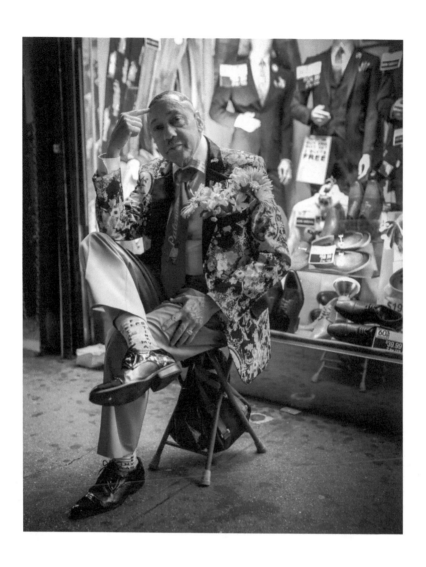

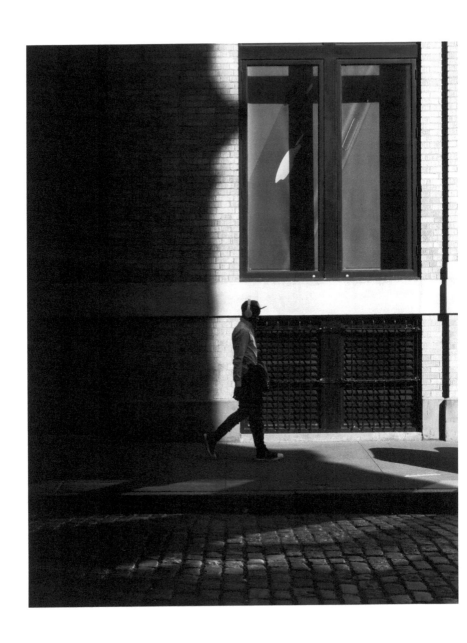

05-22-17 SoHo

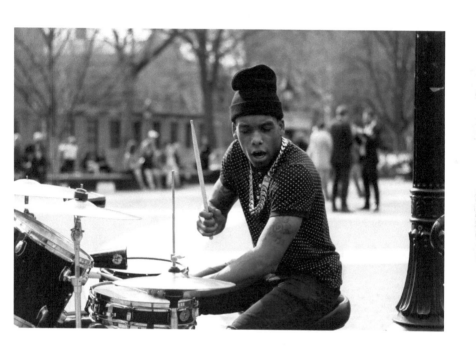

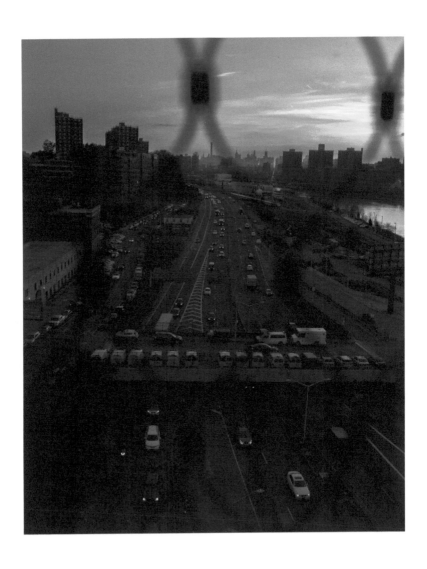

12-01-17 Highbridge

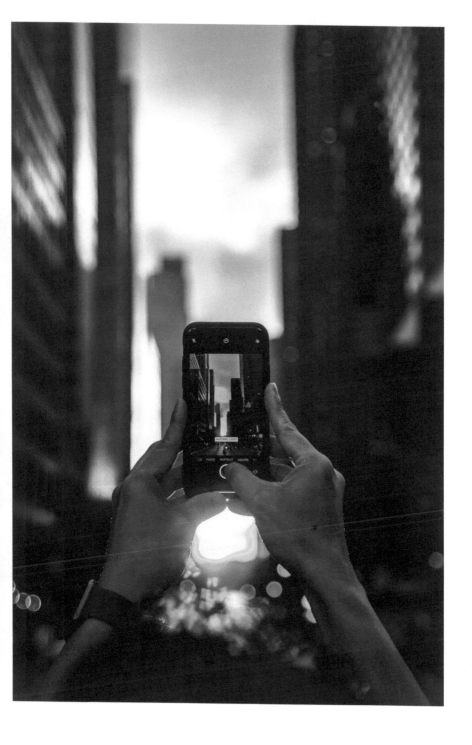

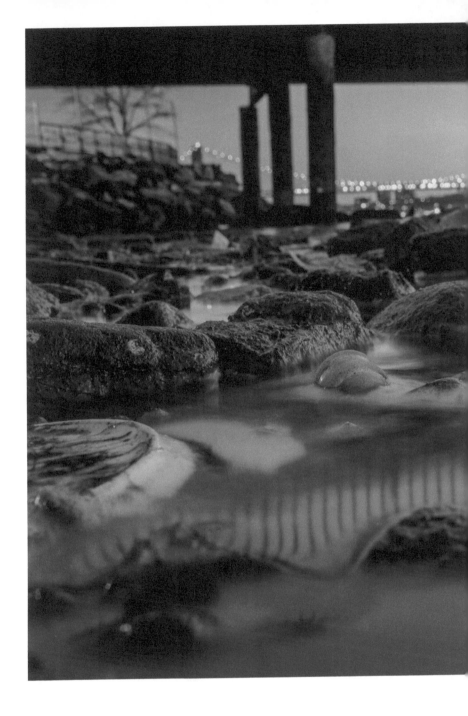

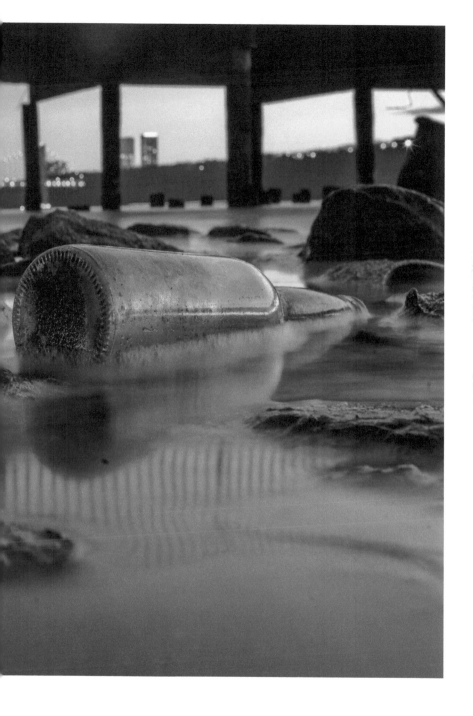

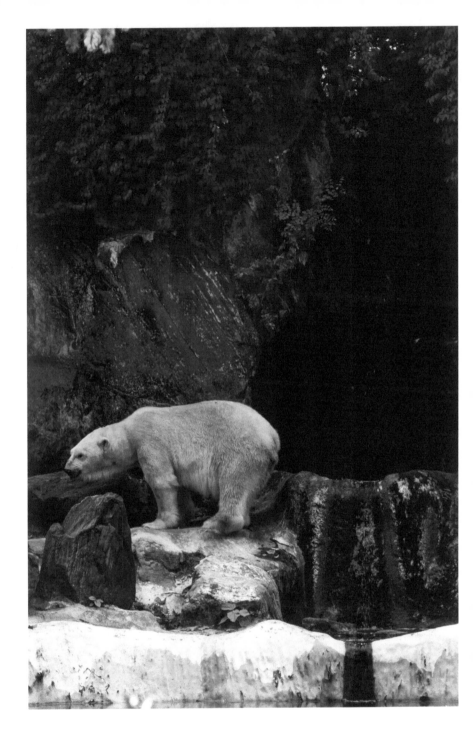

08-18-17 Bronx Zoo

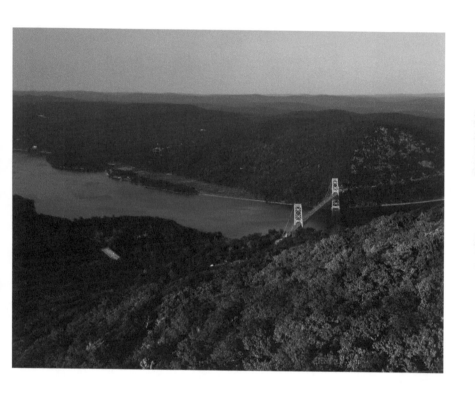

05-24-18 Bear Mountain Bridge

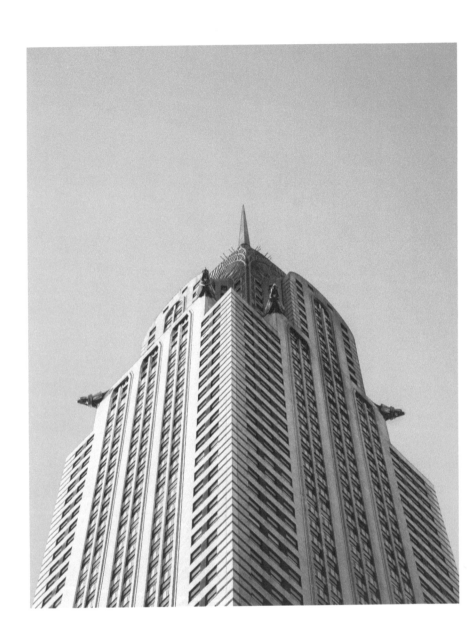

05-30-18 Chrysler Building

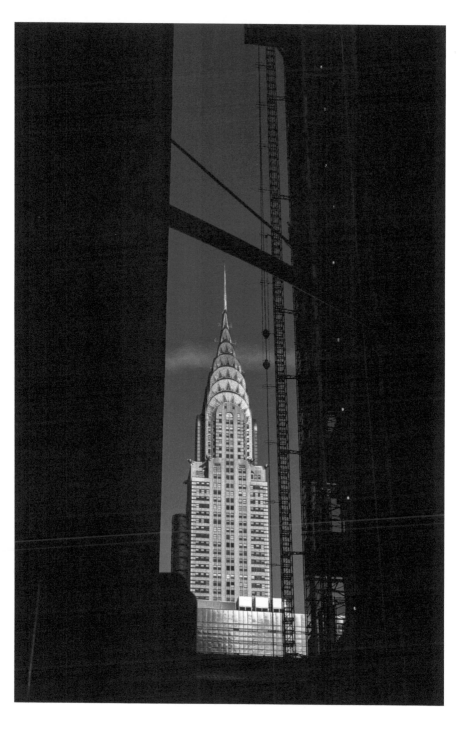

05-30-18 Chrysler Building

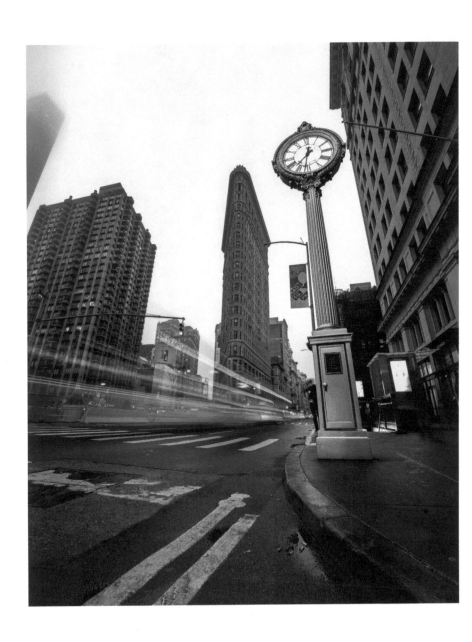

04-30-18 Flatiron District

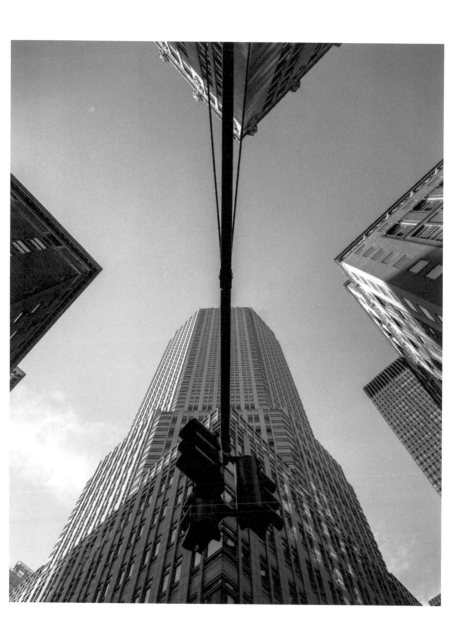

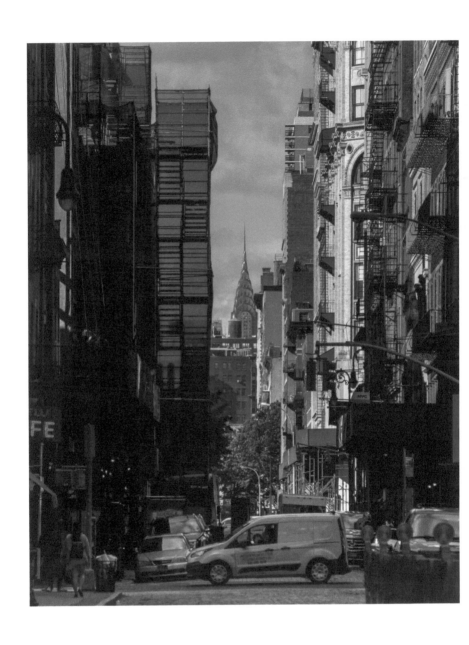

05-22-17 Midtown Manhattan

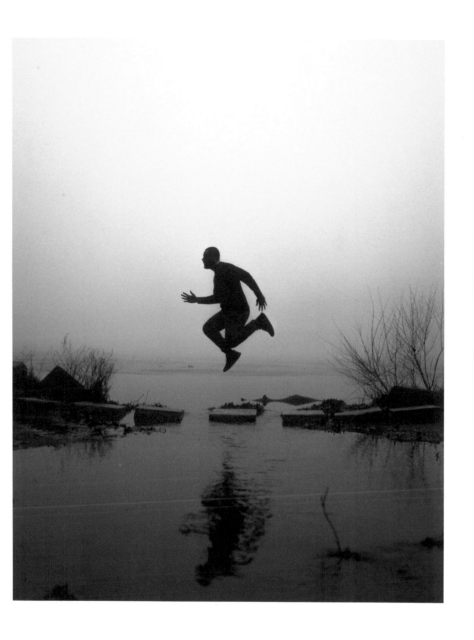

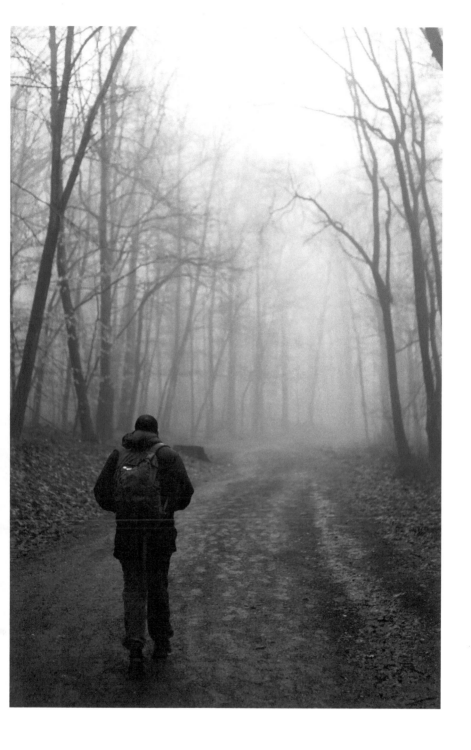

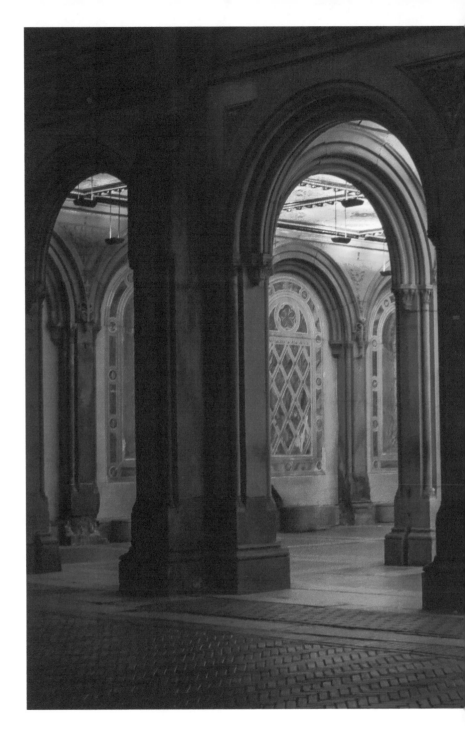

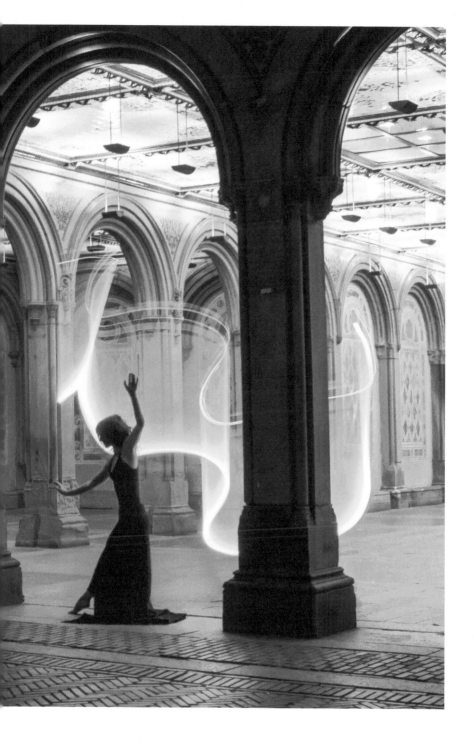

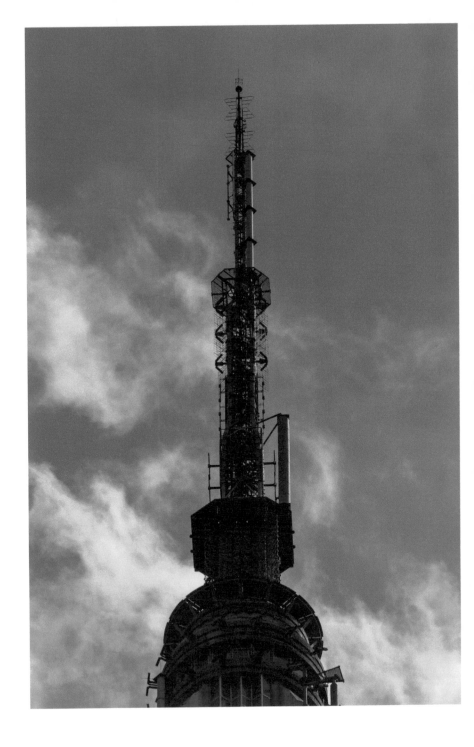

08-18-17 Empire State Building

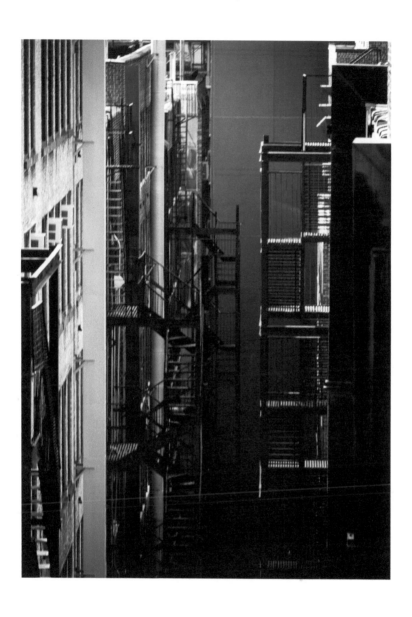

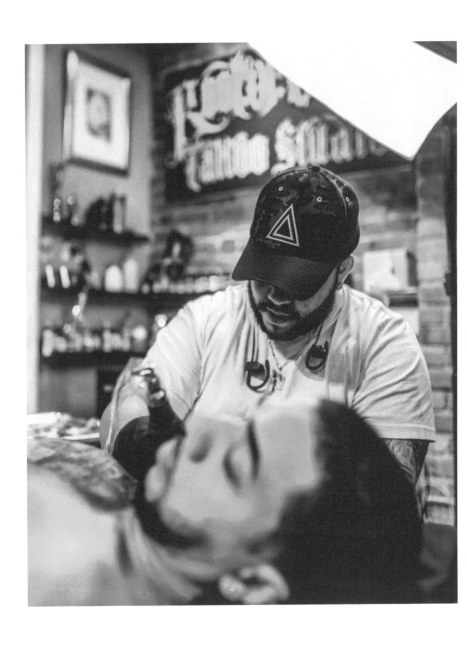

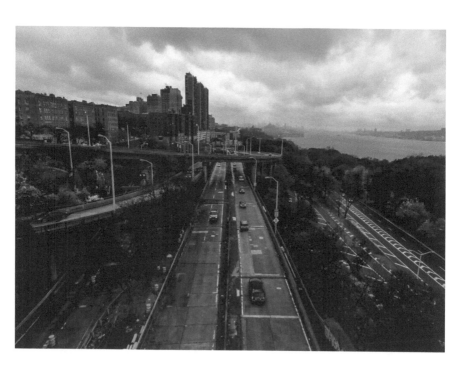

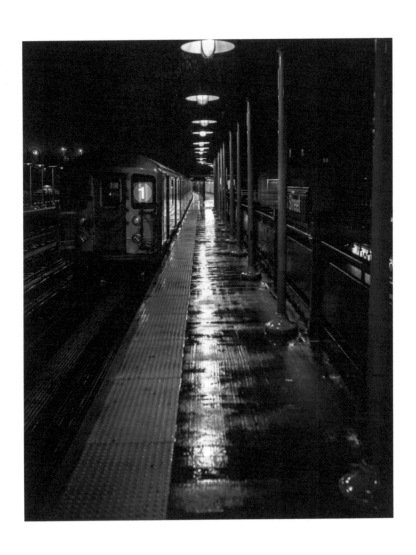

12-05-17 The Bronx

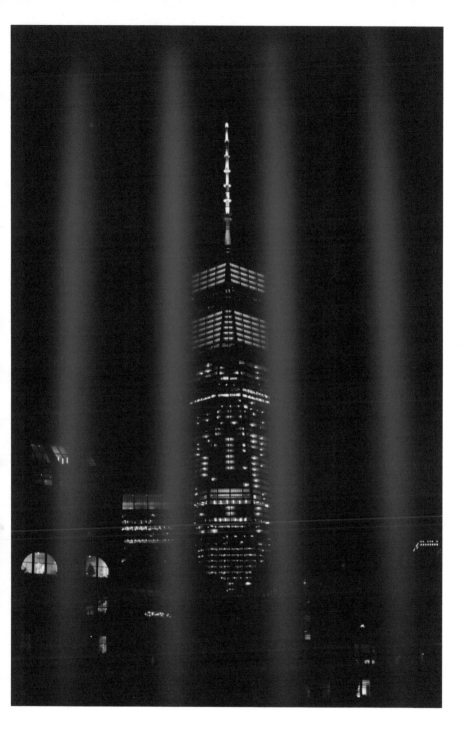

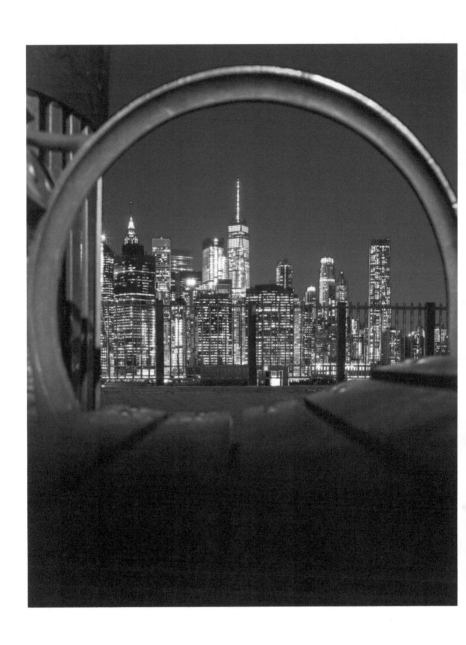

01-28-18 Brooklyn Heights Promenade

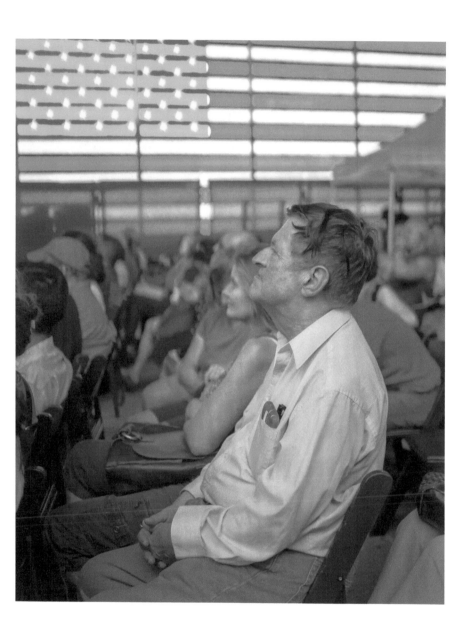

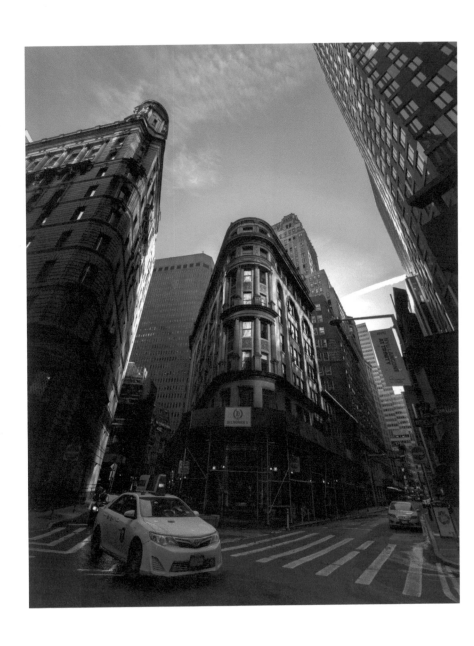

03-22-18 Financial District

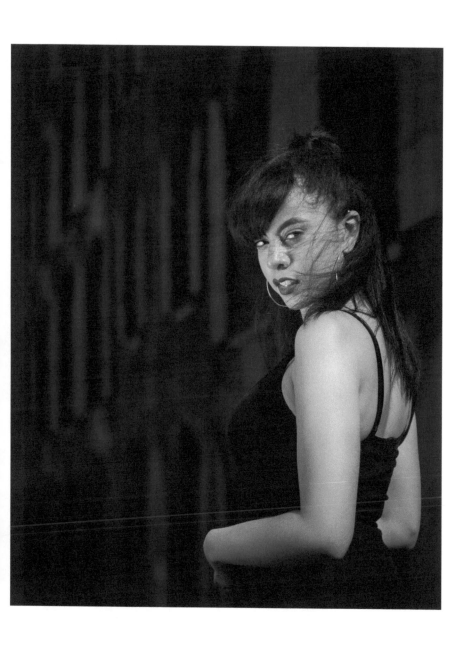

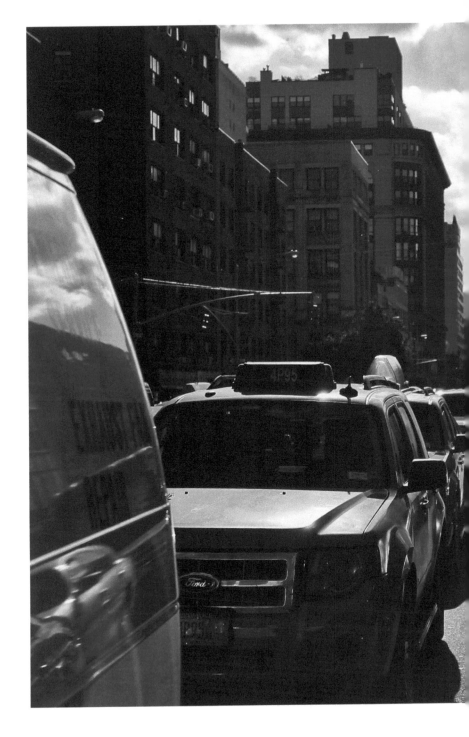

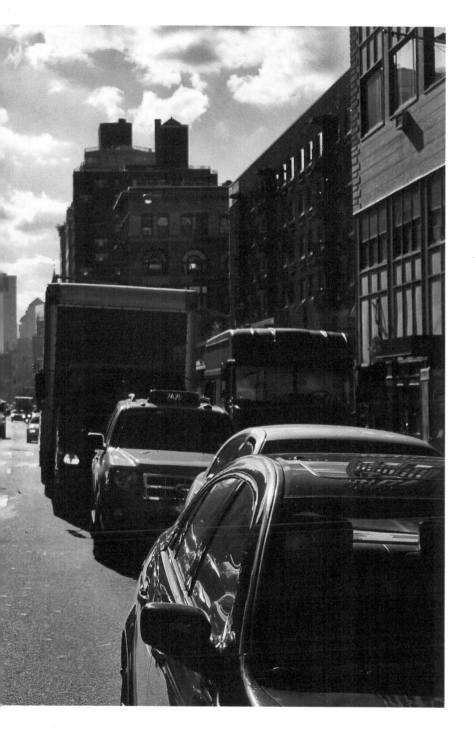

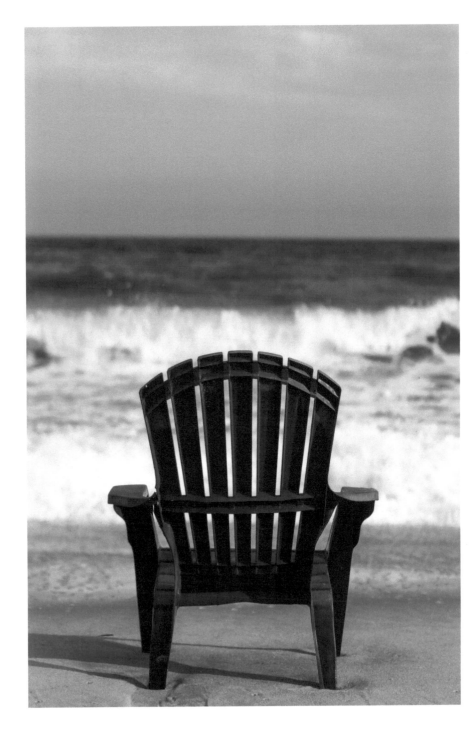

07-09-17 Fire Island

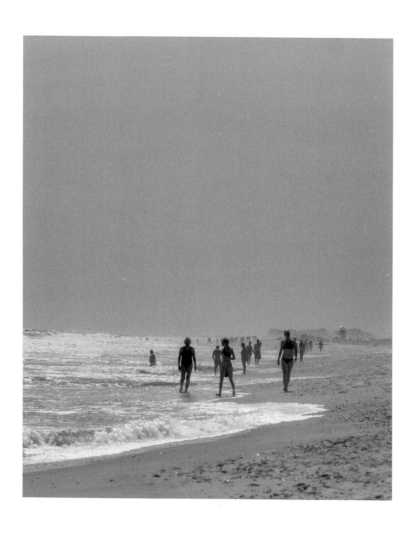

07-09-17 Fire Island

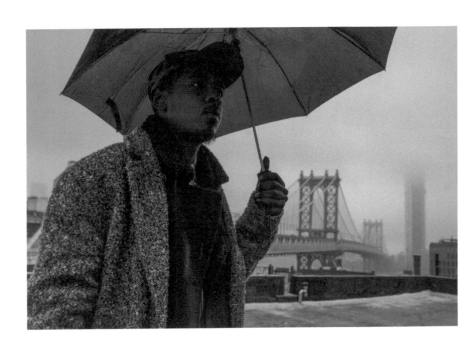

02-07-18 Brooklyn | Hype

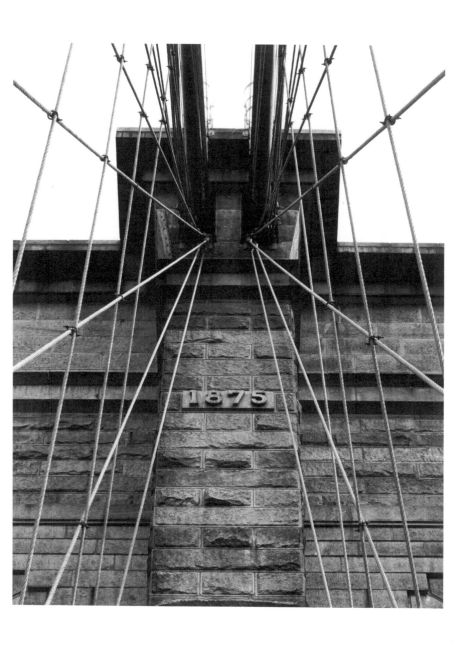

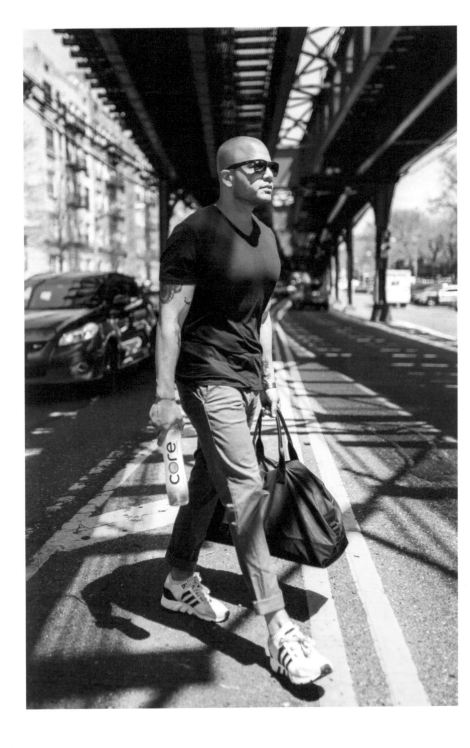

05-04-18 Dyckman | L Boogs

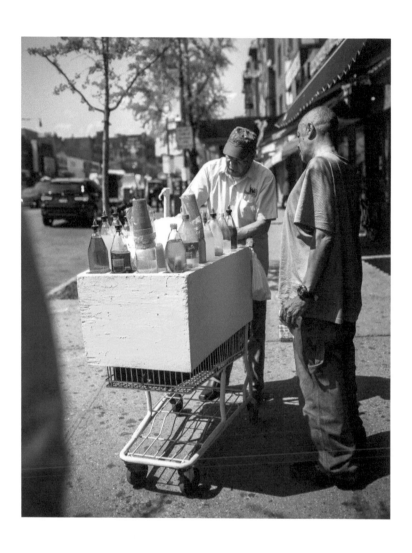

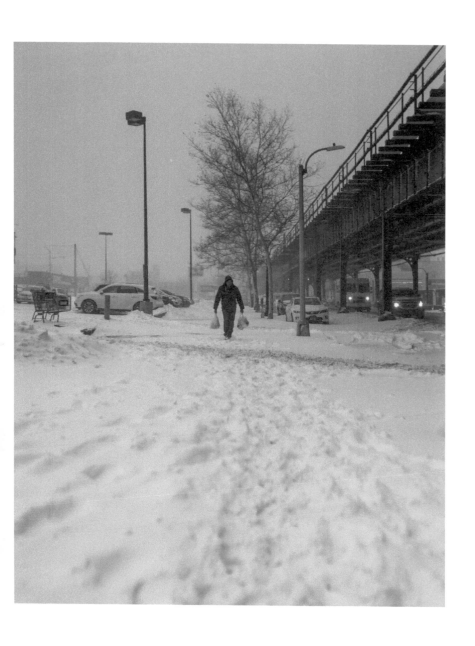

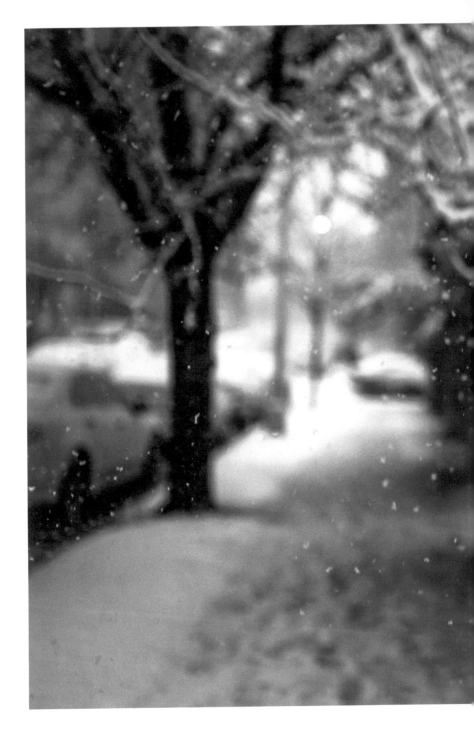

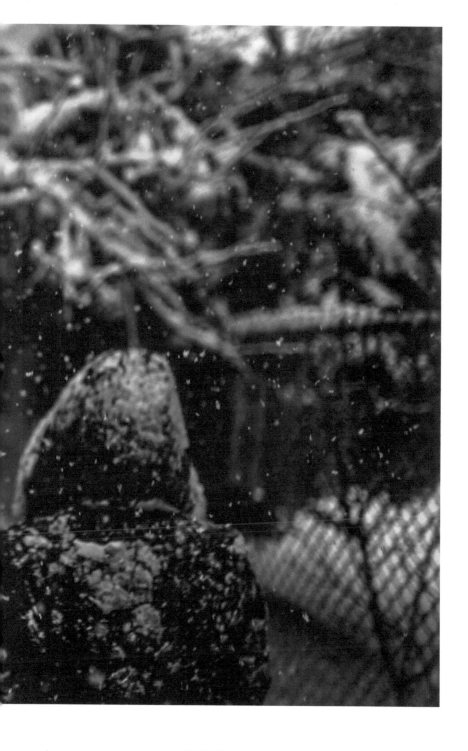

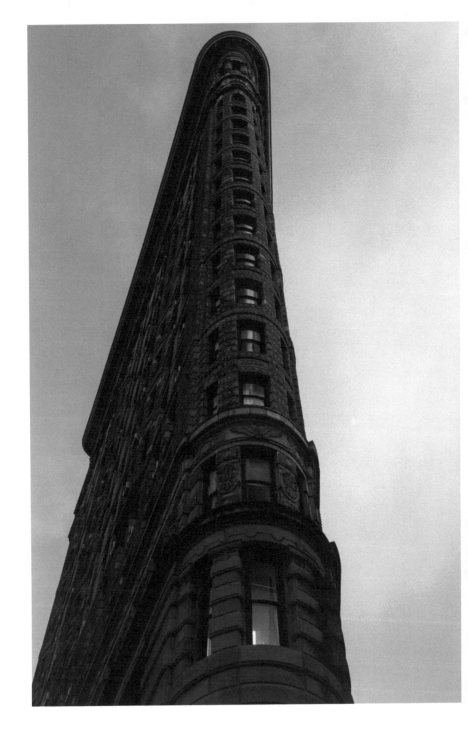

06-02-17 Flatiron Building

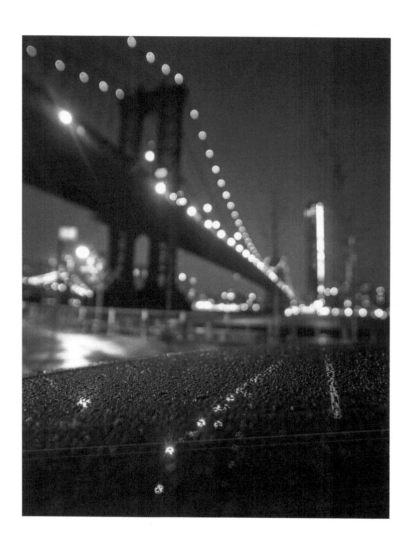

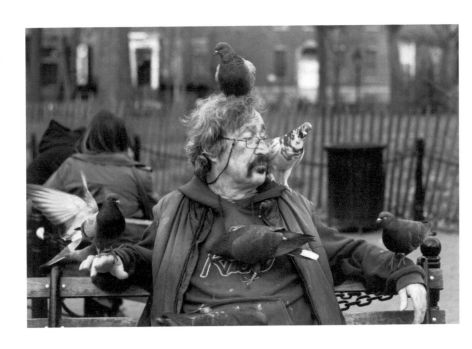

05-31-16 Washington Square Park

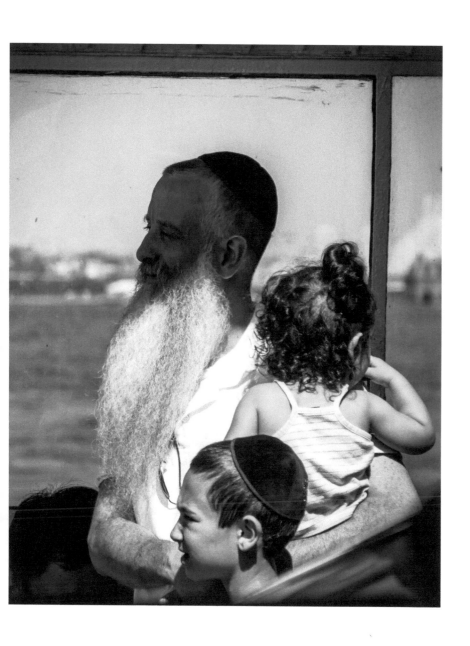

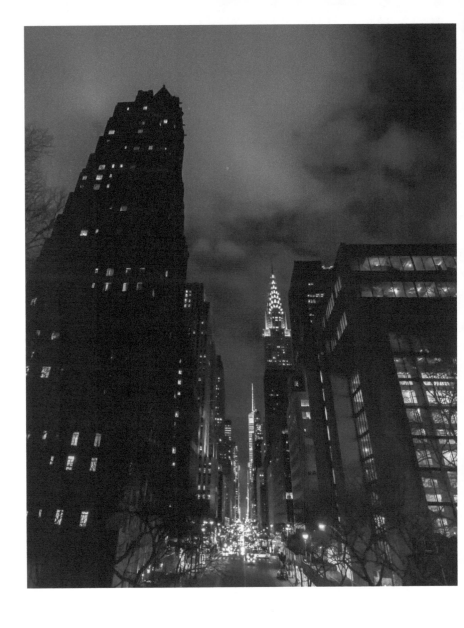

03-25-18 Tudor City

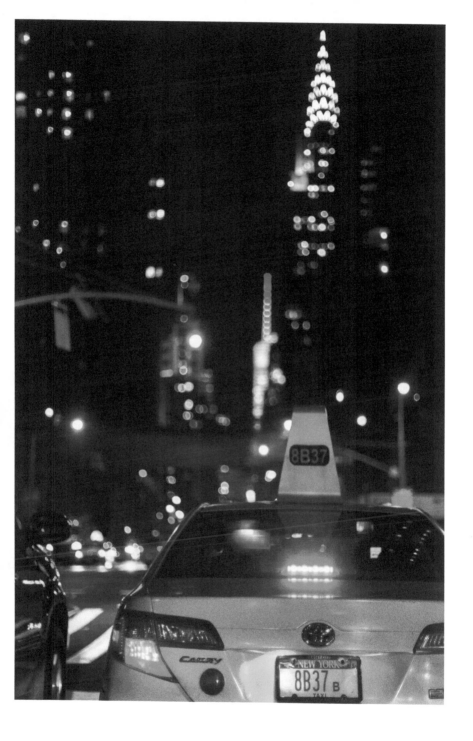

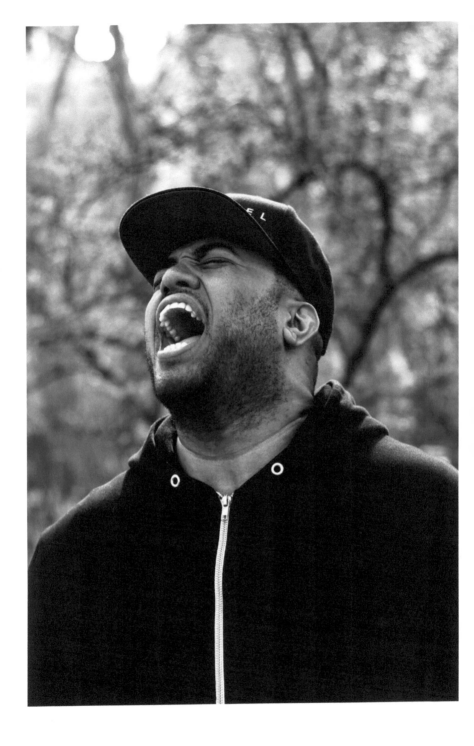

04-01-16 J. Hood Wright Park | Mark Henny

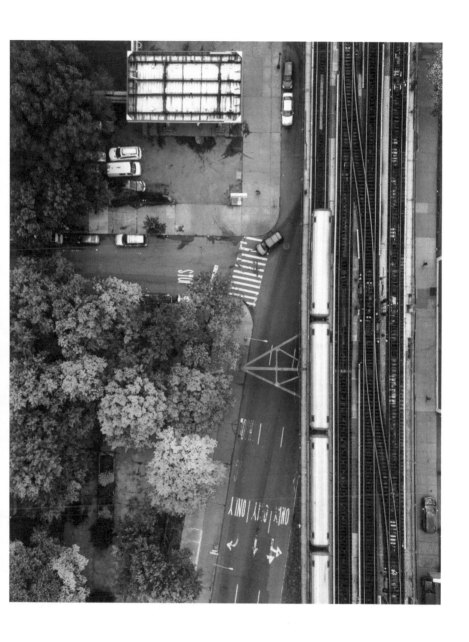

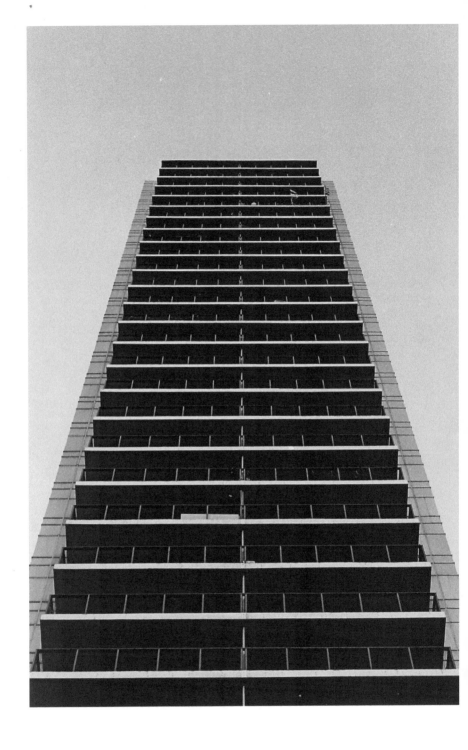

11-14-17 Washington Heights

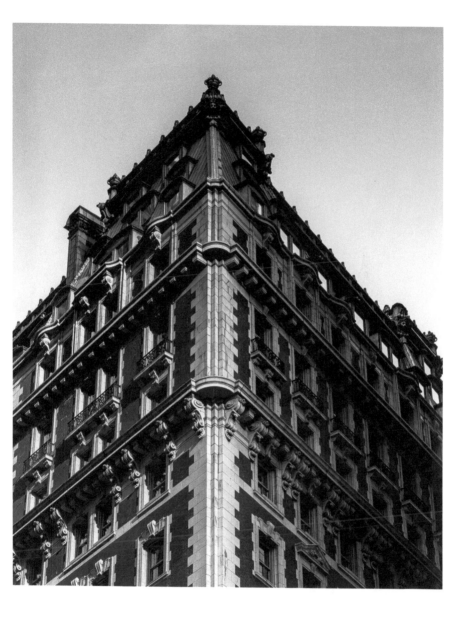

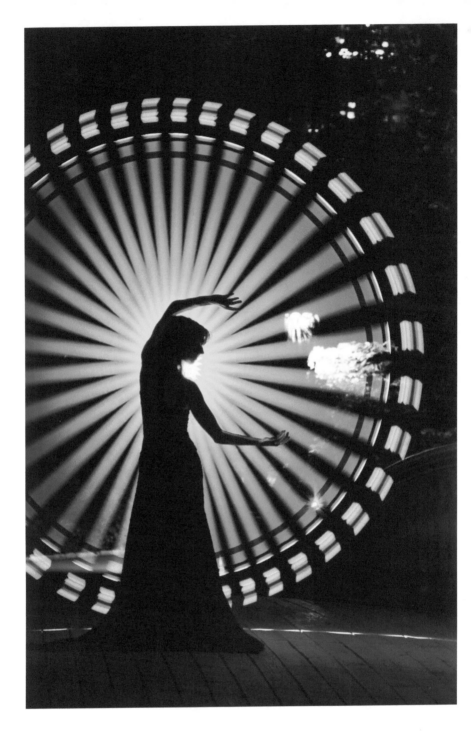

07-31-17 Bow Bridge | Kim Henry | Eric Paré

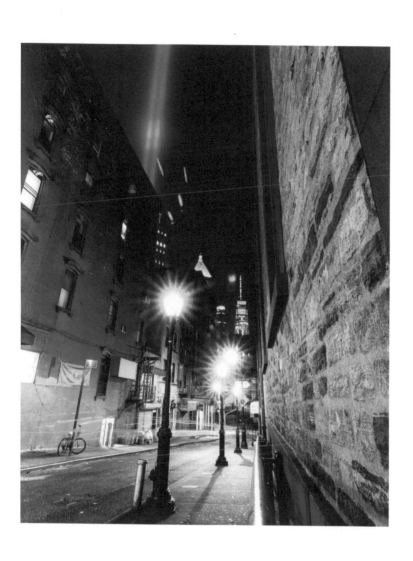

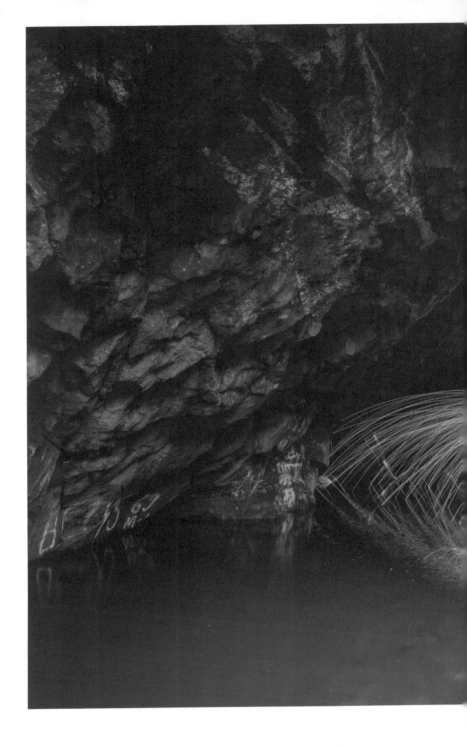

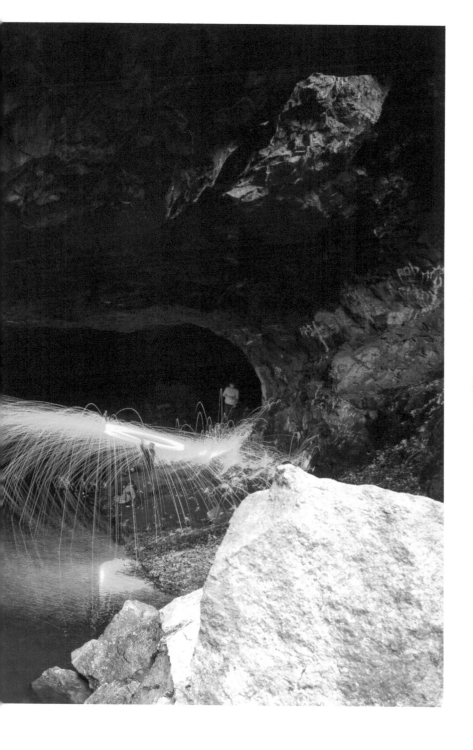

10-04-16 Bear Mountain | Berto

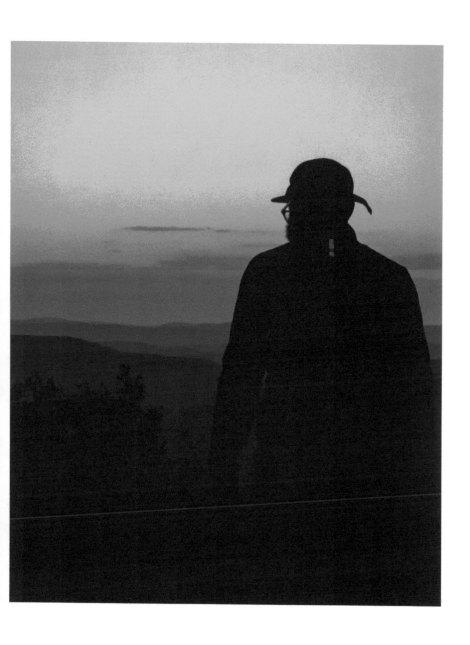

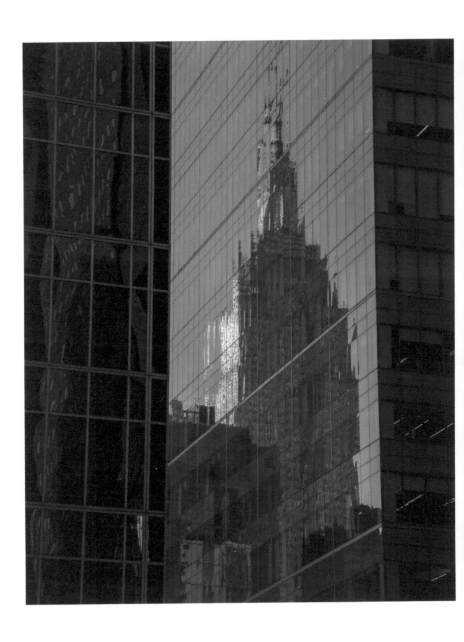

05-30-18 Midtown Manhattan

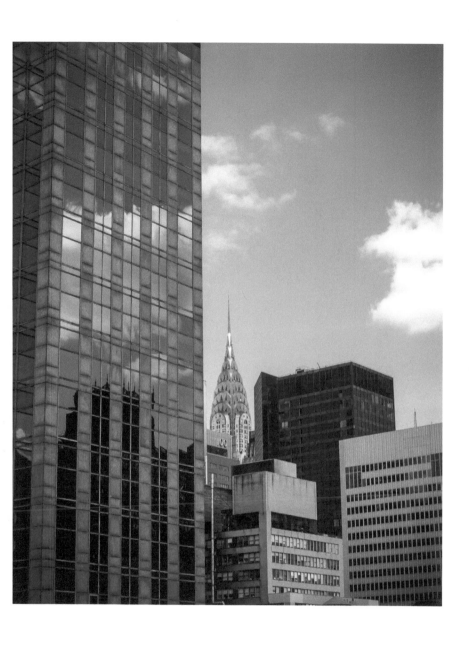

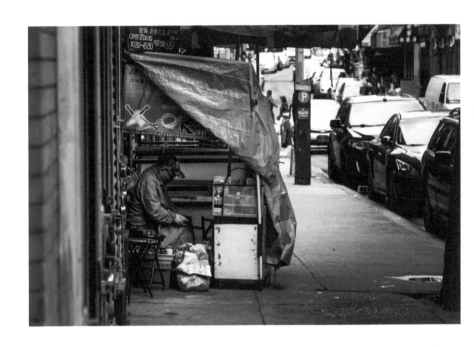

06-08-17 Chinatown

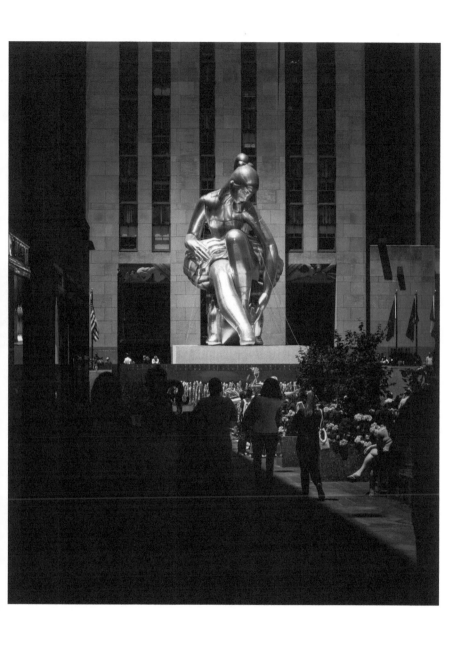

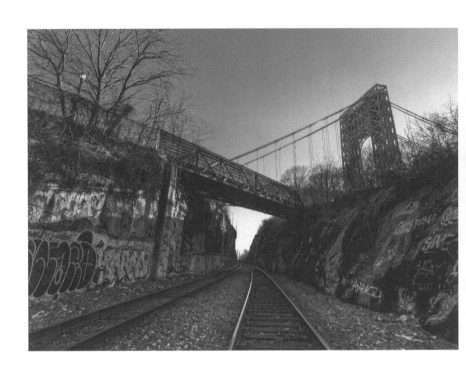

04-14-17 George Washington Bridge

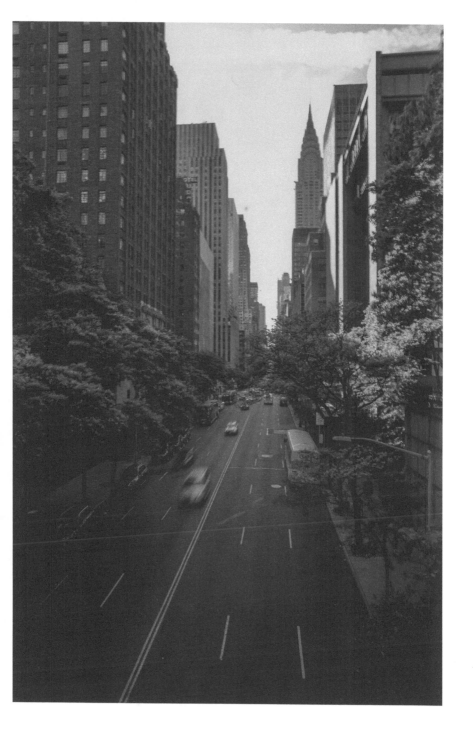

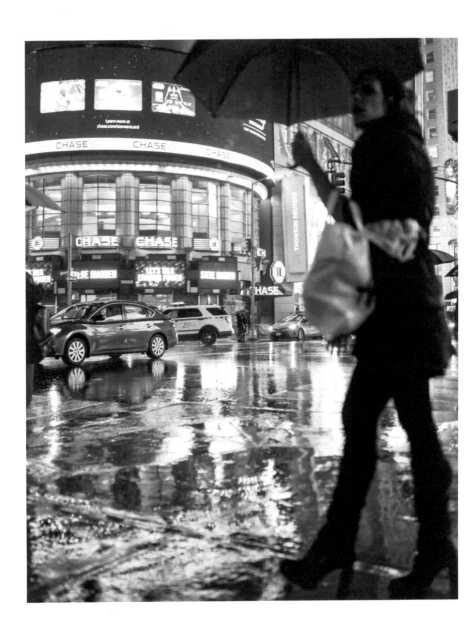

12-05-17 Times Square

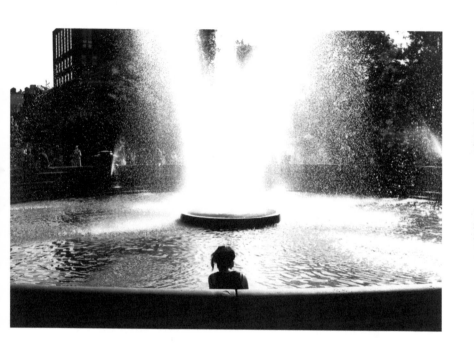

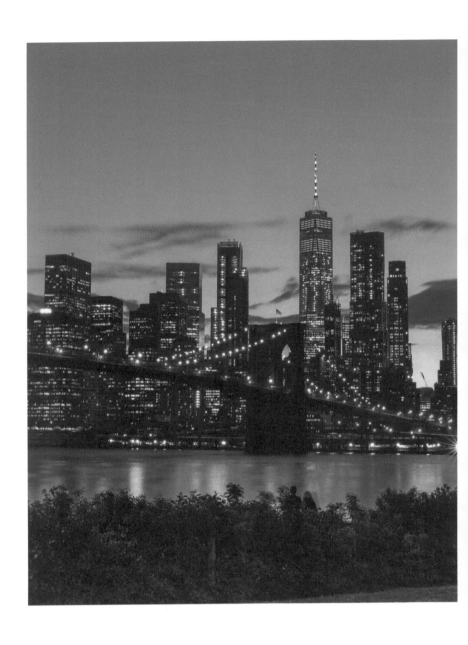

06 04 18 DUMBO

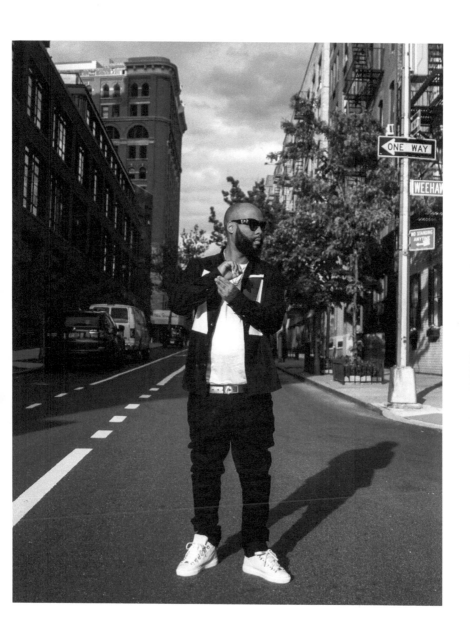

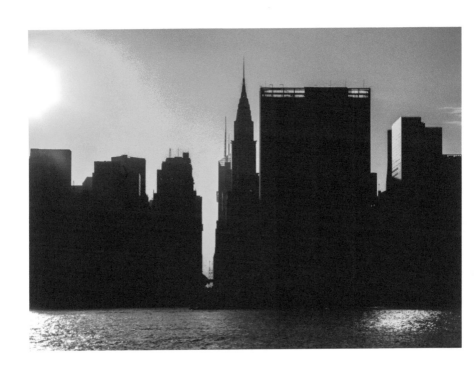

05-29-18 Long Island City

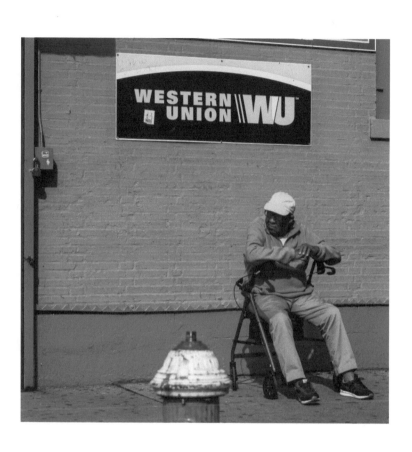

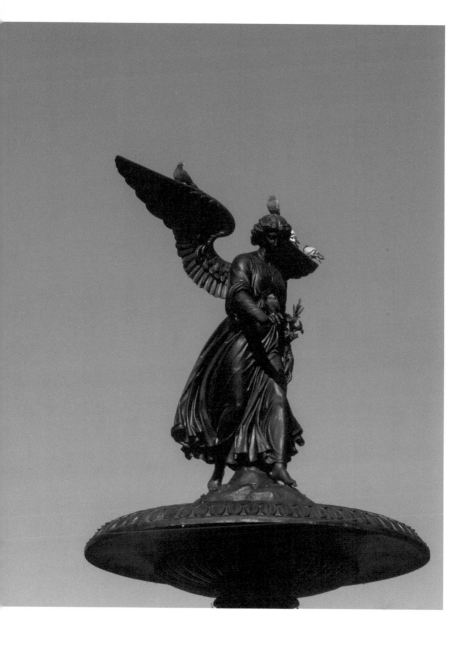

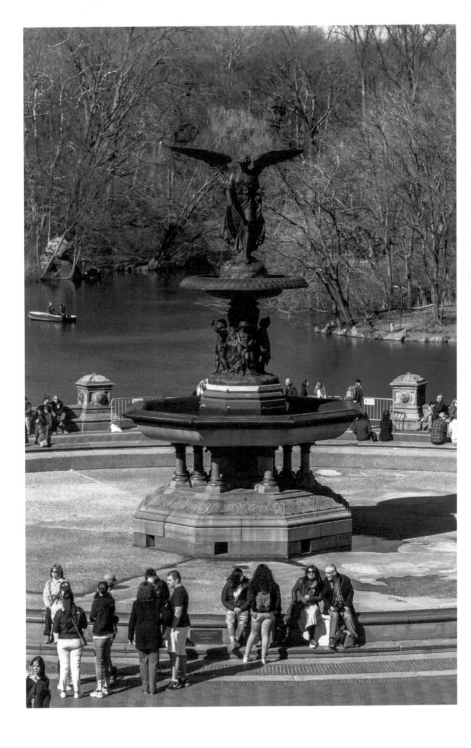

05-22-17 Bethesda Fountain

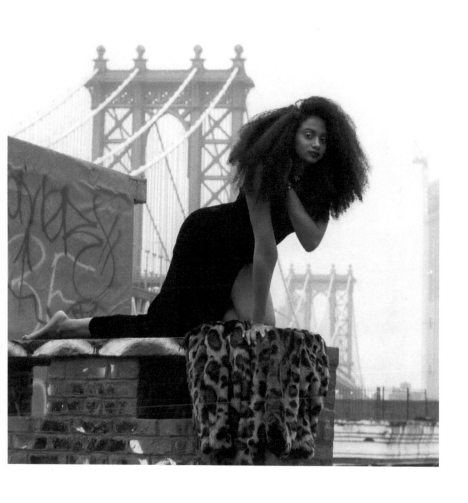

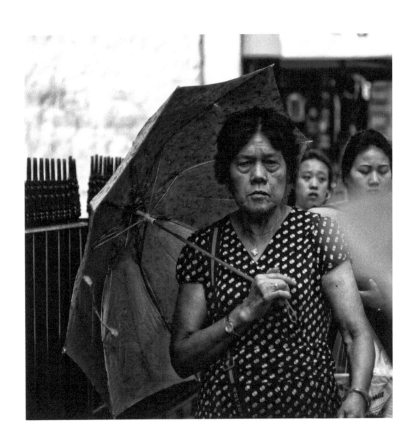

08-22-16 Chinatown

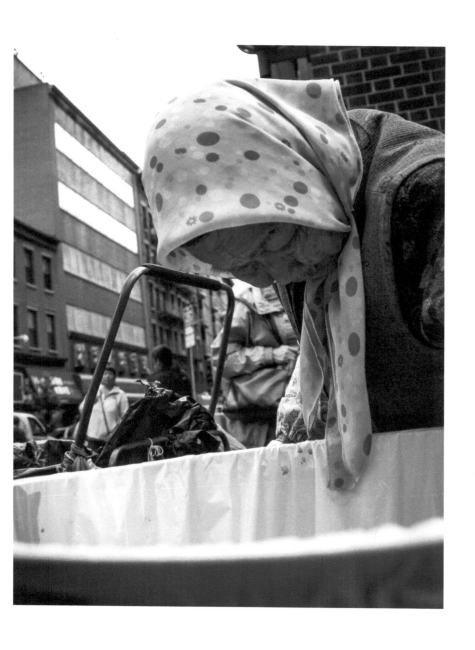

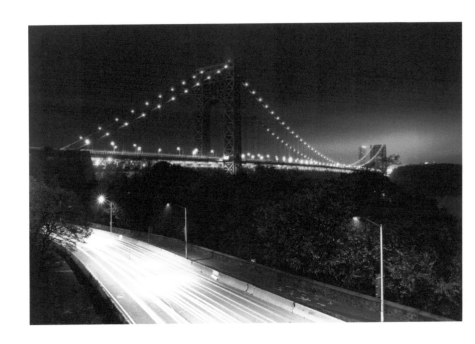

10-27-16 George Washington Bridge

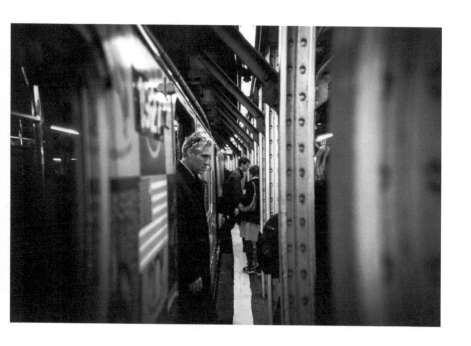

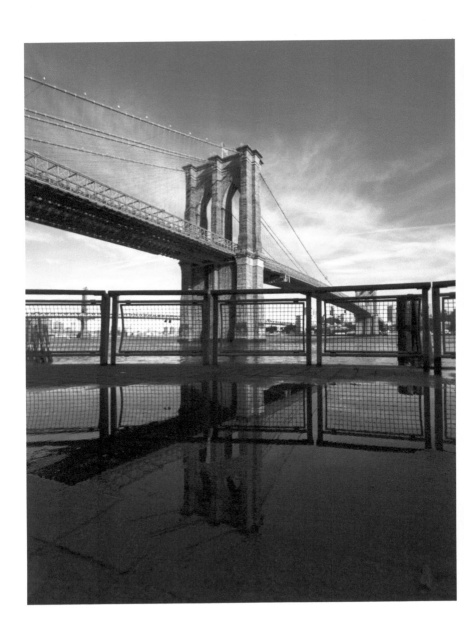

03-22-18 Brooklyn Bridge

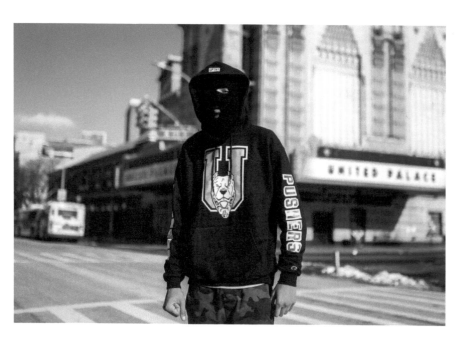

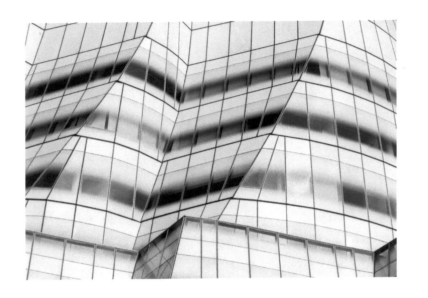

09·14·16 Chelsea

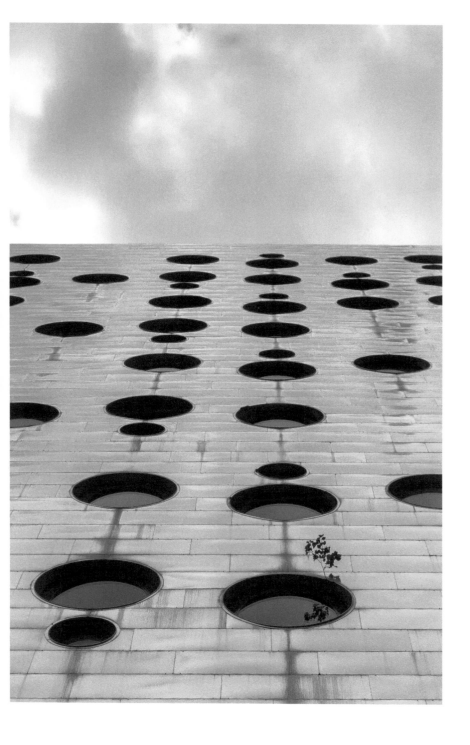

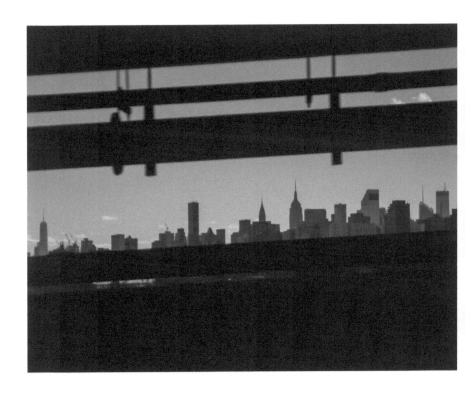

04·03·16 Triboro Bridge

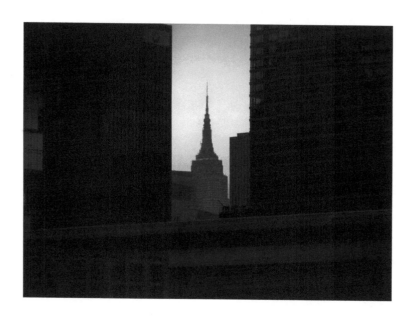

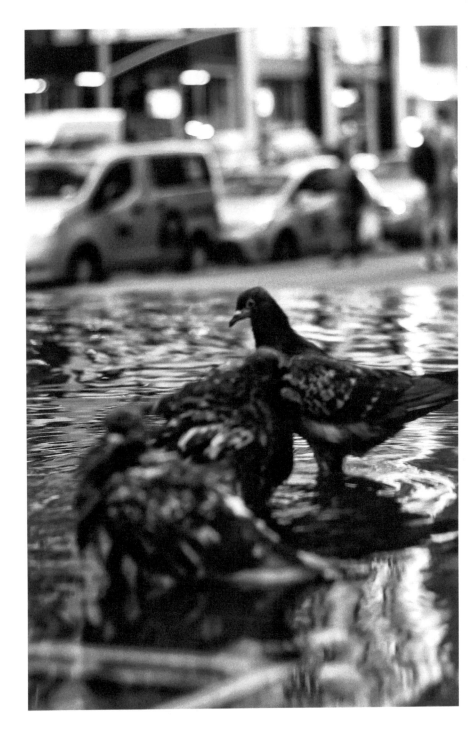

09-13-16 Radio City

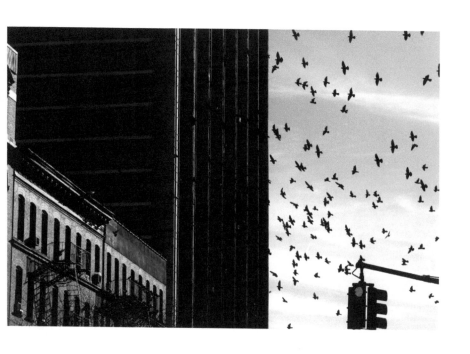

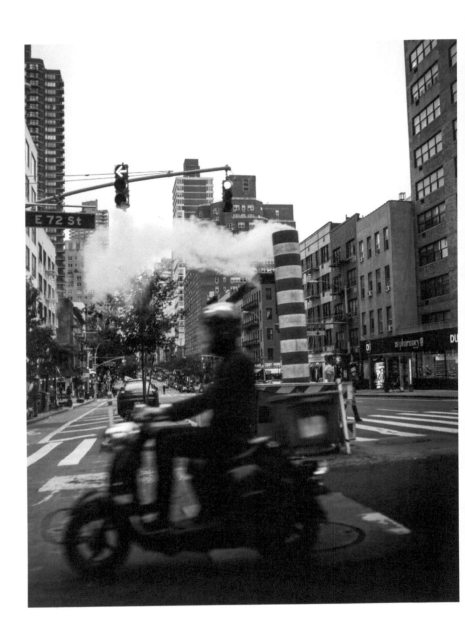

11-26-17 Gramercy

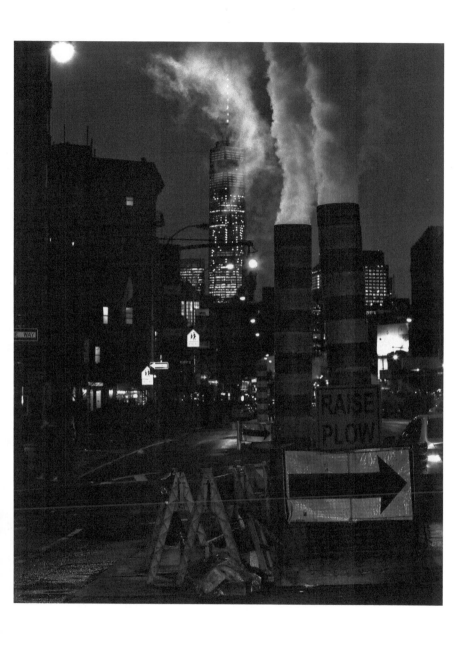

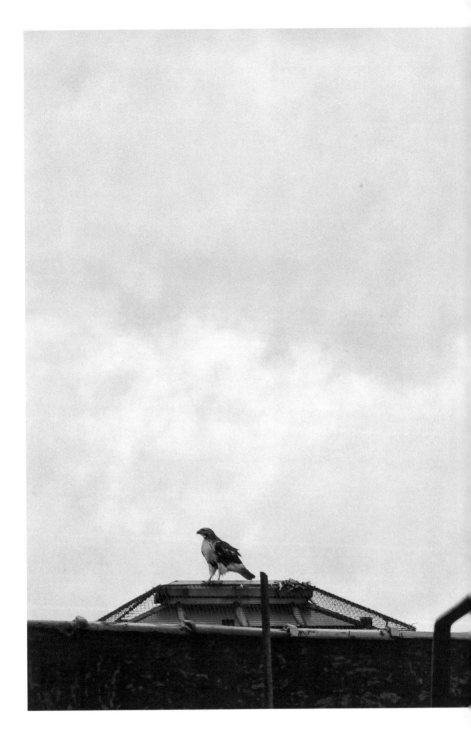

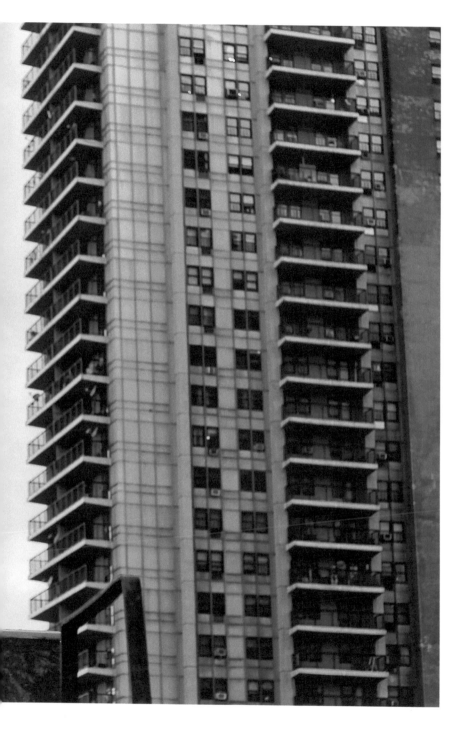

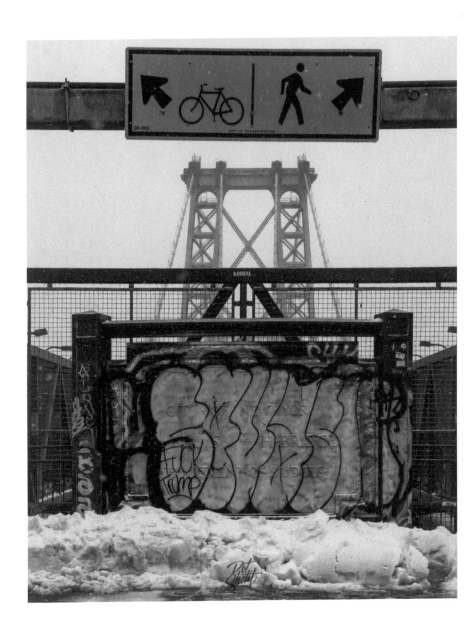

03-14-17 Williamsburg

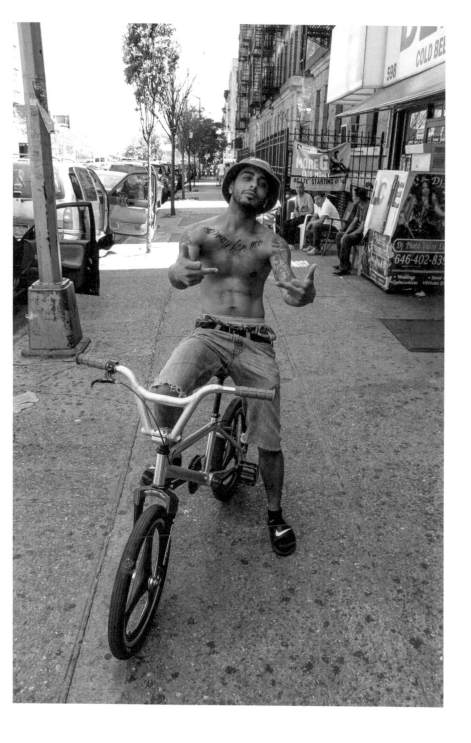

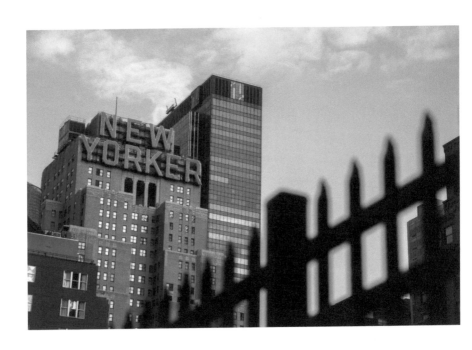

06·04·18 Wyndham New Yorker Hotel

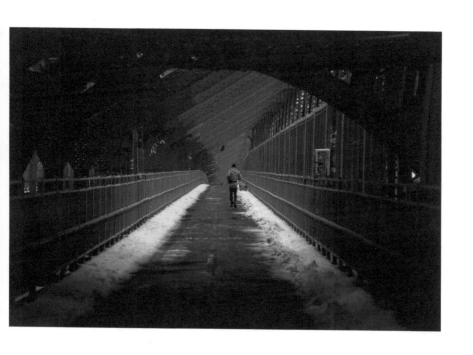

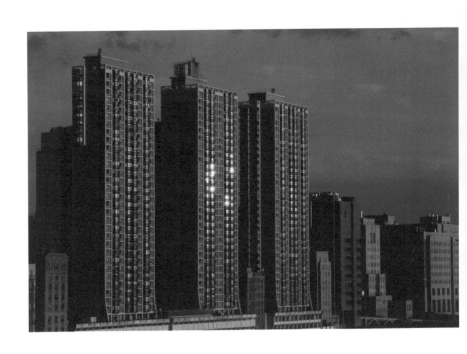

08·08·16 Washington Heights

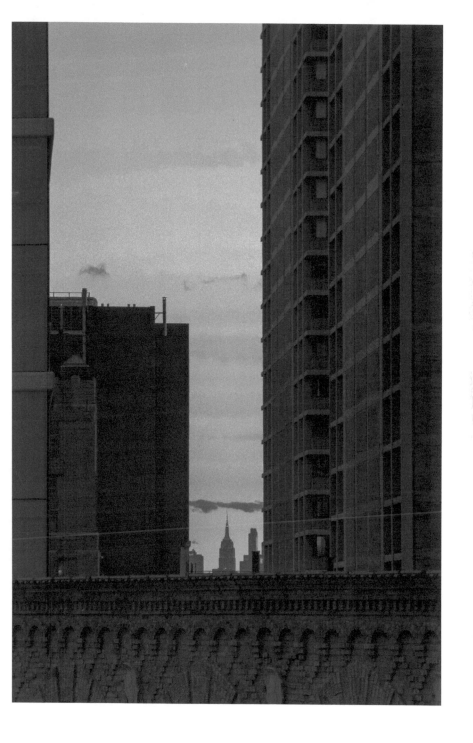

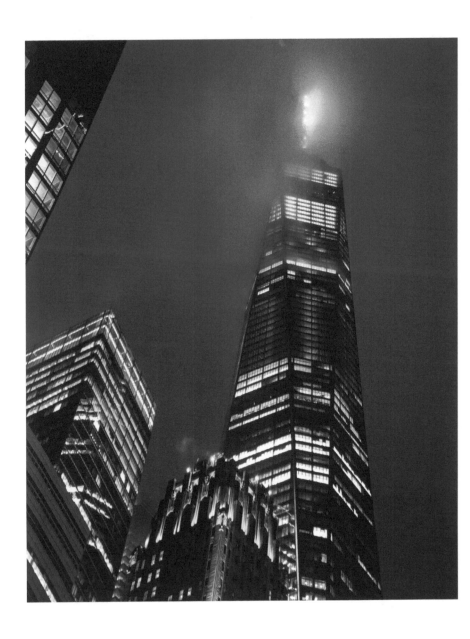

02-27-18 One World Trade

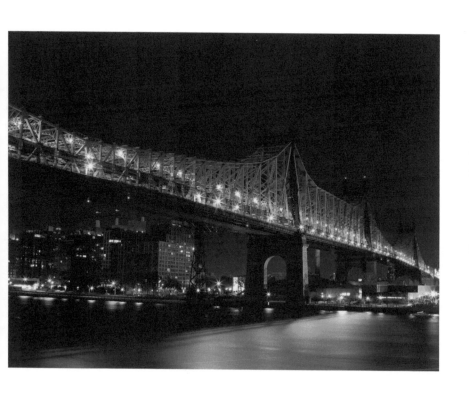

11-16-15 Ed Koch Queensboro Bridge

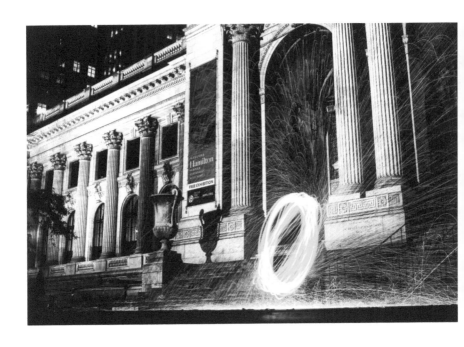

10-31-16 New York Public Library

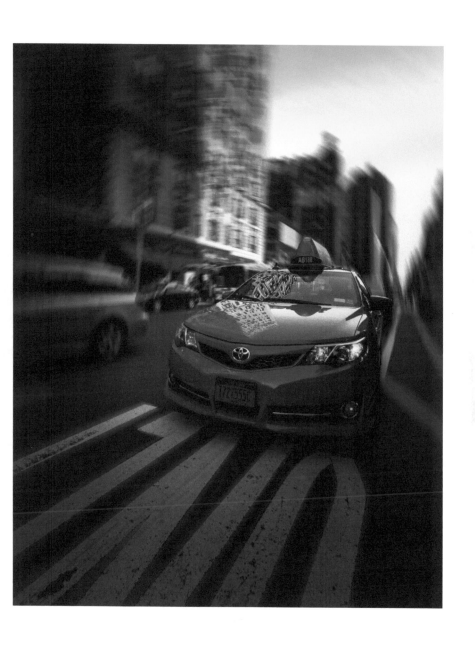

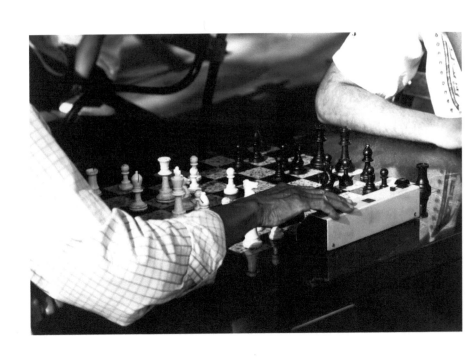

08-22-16 Washington Square Park

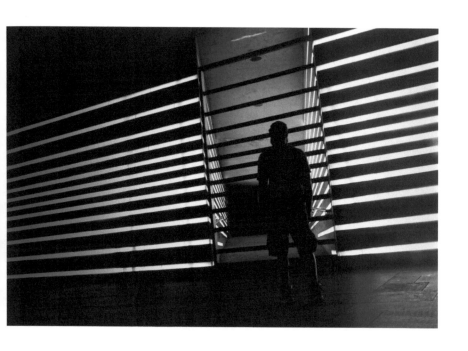

09-17-16 Canal Street

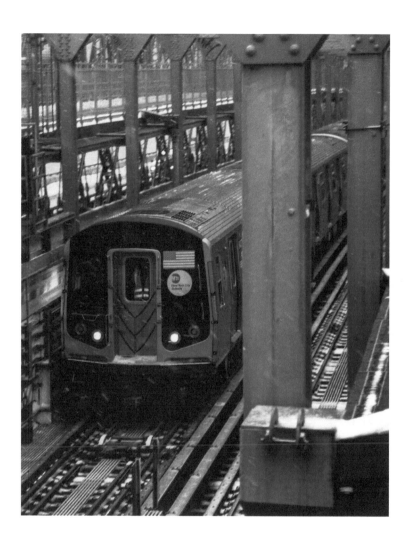

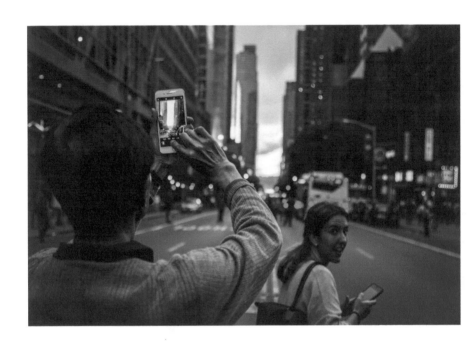

05-30-18 Manhattanhenge

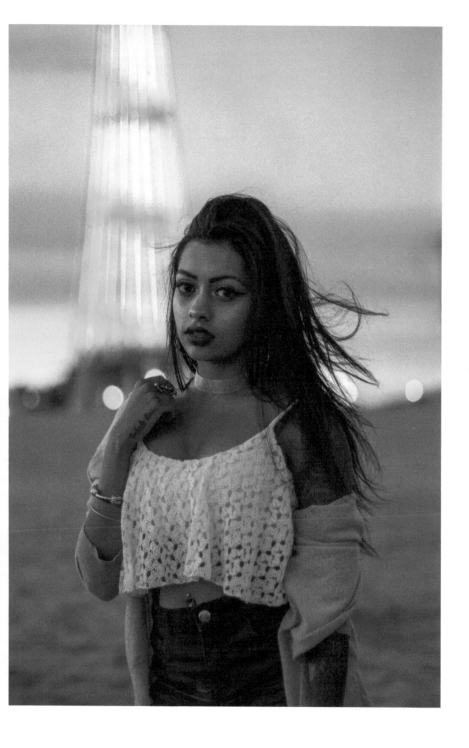

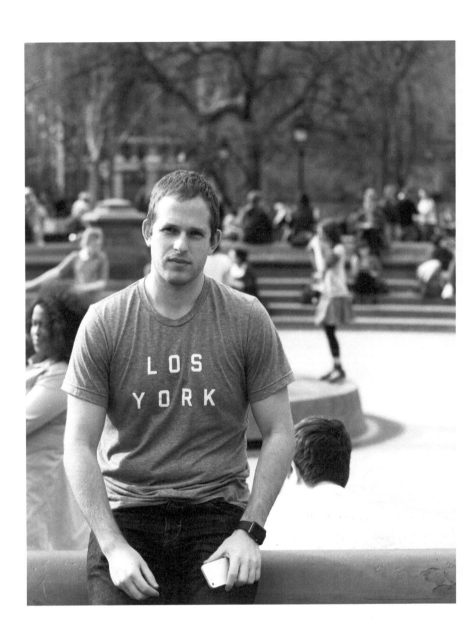

05·31·16 Washington Square Park

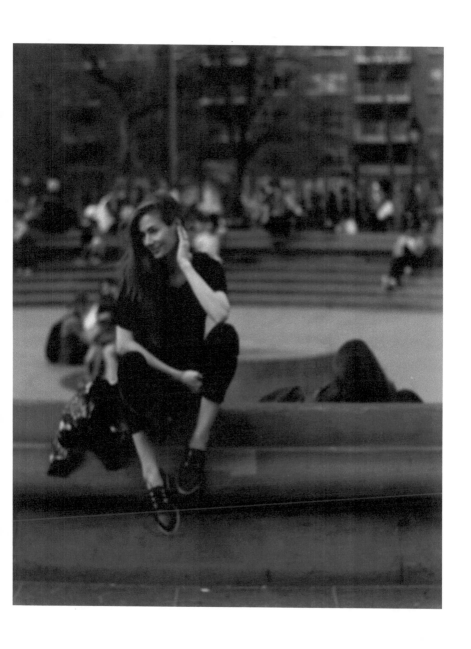

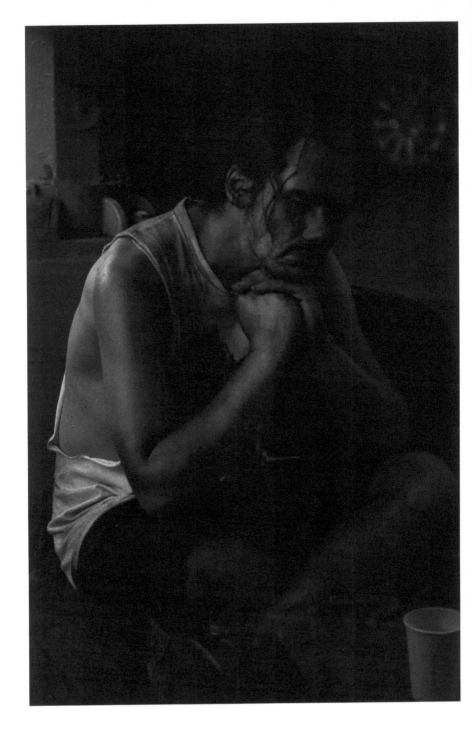

08-29-16 Times Square

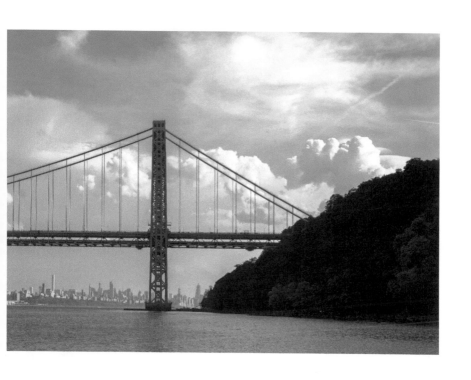

05-26-18 George Washington Bridge

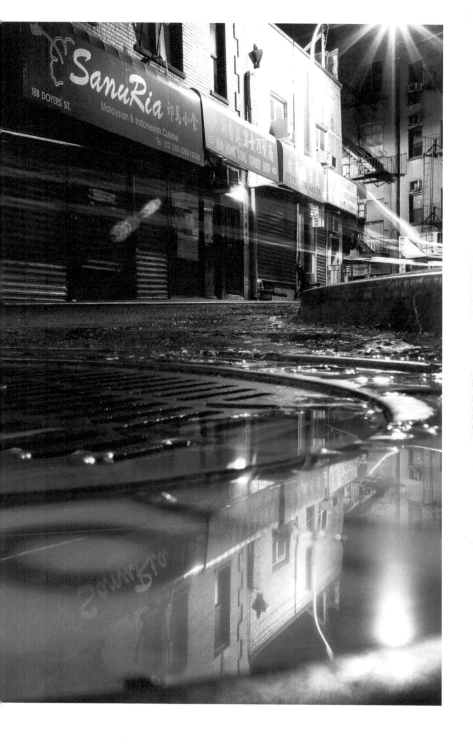

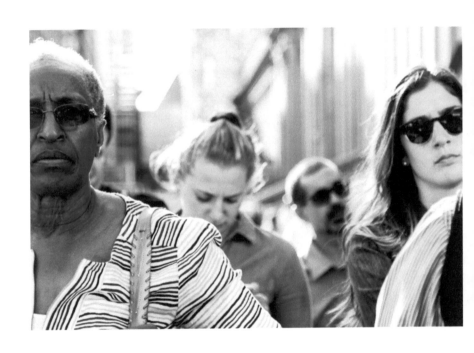

06-22-17 Downtown Manhattan

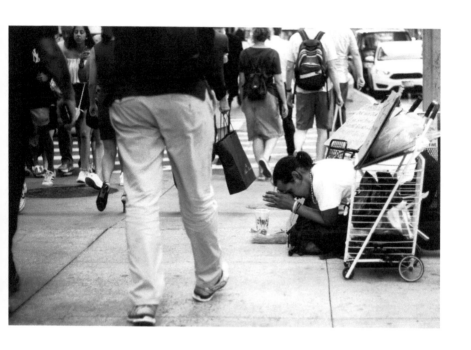

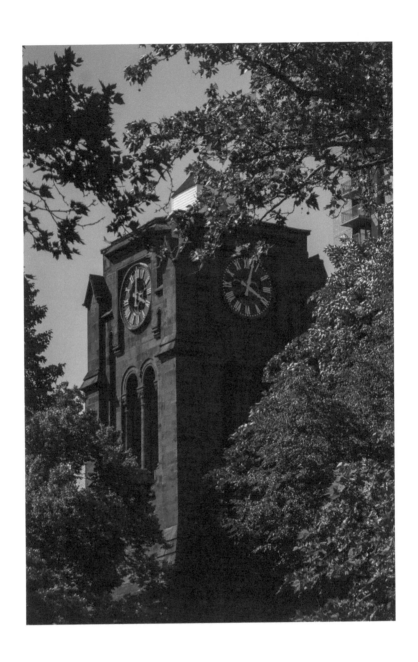

05-30-18 Gramercy

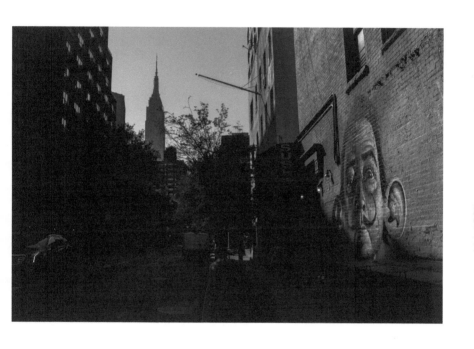

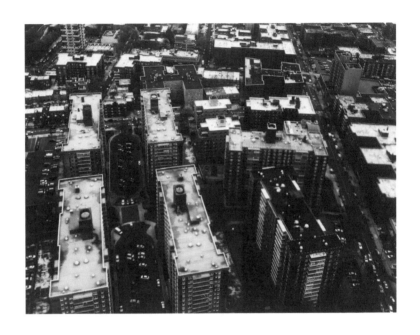

01-08-16 Queens

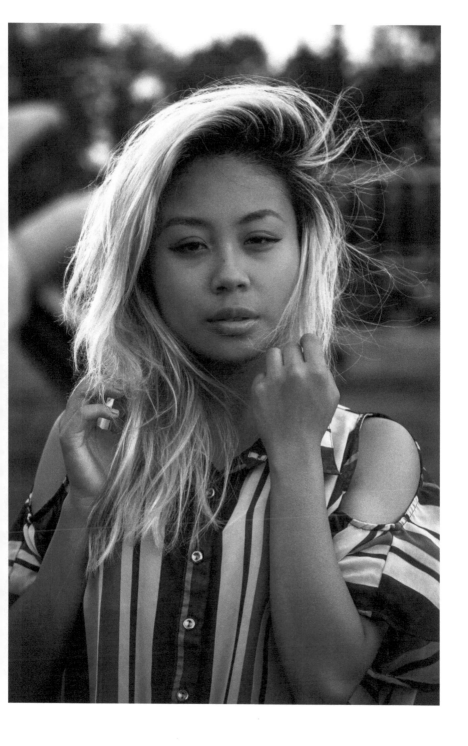

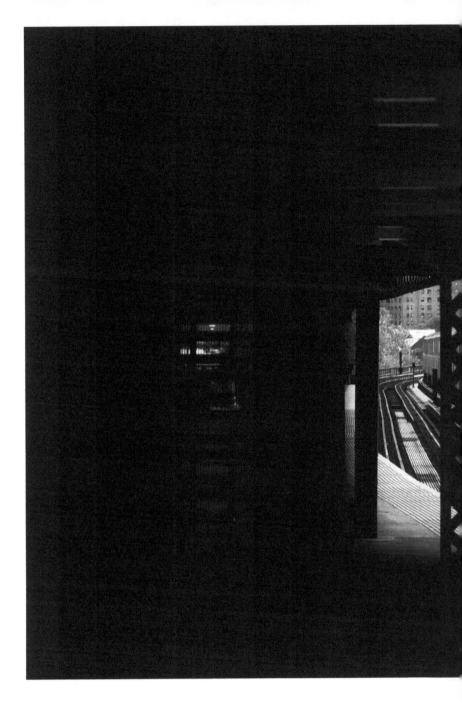

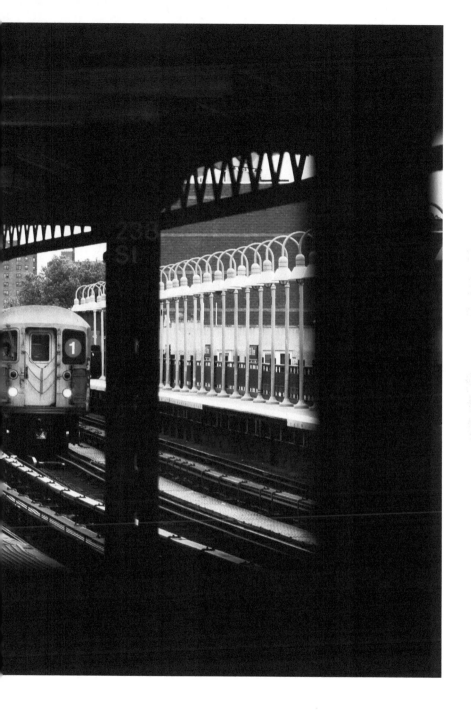

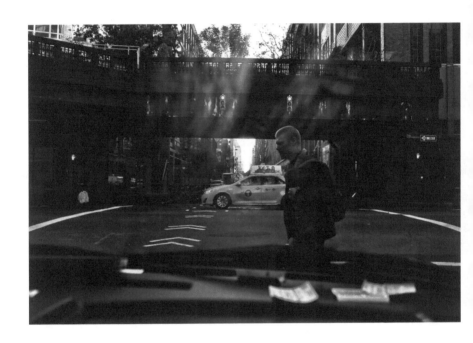

01-21-16 Chelsea

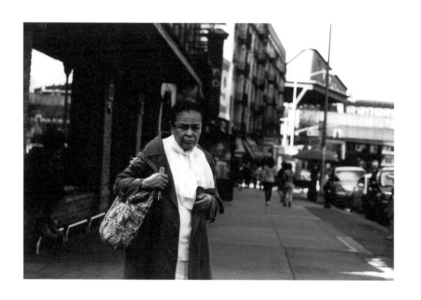

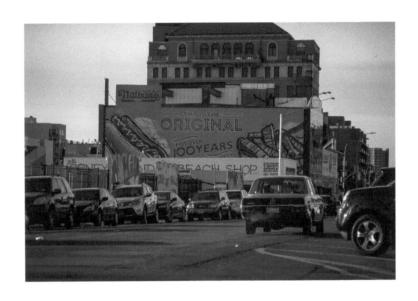

05-14-17 Coney Island

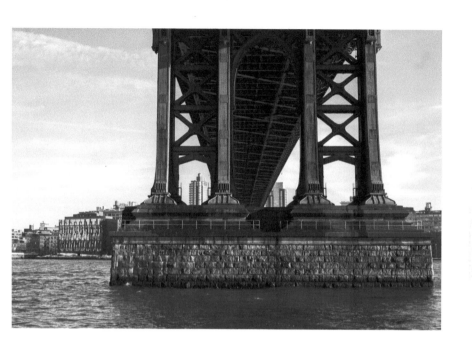

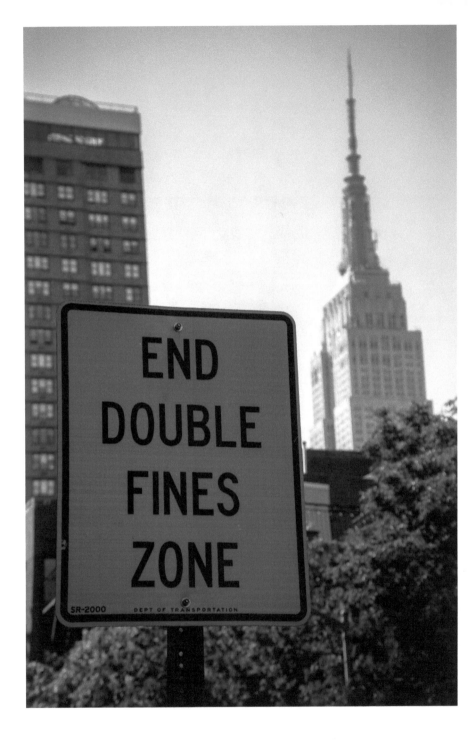

05-30-18 Midtown Manhattan

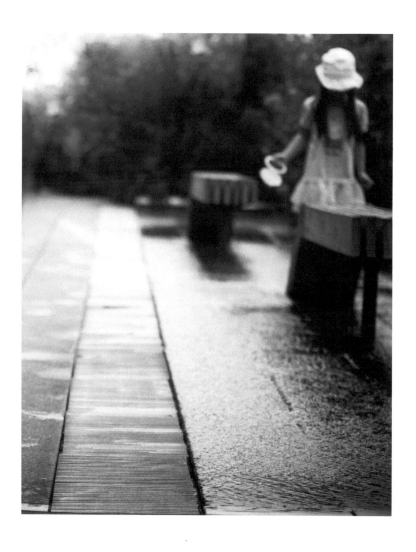

07/27/17 The High Line

If you got to this page, **thank you**!

I shot these for you.

ISBN 978-0692156650

All photographs by Jeffrey "DotShotIt" Batista
Book Design by Jean Goode

Printed and bound in the United States of America
First Printing June 2018
Second Printing May 2021

Contact dotshotit@icloud.com
Visit www.dotshotit.com

CPSIA information can be obtained
at www.ICGtesting.com
Printed in the USA
LVHW071655230621
690956LV00001B/149